UEA Scriptwriting Anthology 2013

First published by Egg Box Publishing 2013

International © 2013 retained by individual authors

This book is sold subject to the condition that it shall not, by way of trade or otherwise, be lent, resold, hired out, stored in a retrieval system, or otherwise circulated without the publisher's prior consent in any form of binding or cover other than that in which it is published and without a similar condition including this condition being imposed on the subsequent purchaser.

A CIP record for this book is available from the British Library.

UEA Scriptwriting Anthology 2013 is typeset in 10pt Caslon, with 13pt leading. Titles in Din, of various weights.

Printed and bound in the UK by Imprint Digital.

Designed and typeset by Sean Purdy.

Cover photography by Christopher Corby.

Proofread by Sarah Gooderson.

Distributed by Central Books.

ISBN: 9780957661127

# Acknowledgements

Thanks are due to the School of Literature, Drama and Creative Writing at UEA in partnership with Egg Box Publishing for making this anthology possible.

We'd also like to thank the following people:

Moniza Alvi, Amit Chaudhuri, Andrew Cowan, William Fiennes, Giles Foden, Sarah Gooderson, Lavinia Greenlaw, Rachel Hore, Kathryn Hughes, Katie Konyn, Daniel Leeson, Michael Lengsfield, Jean McNeil, Natalie Mitchell, Beatrice Poubeau, Rob Ritchie, Michèle Roberts, James Scudamore, Ali Smith, Helen Smith, Henry Sutton, George Szirtes, Val Taylor, Steve Waters and Peter Womack.

Nathan Hamilton at Egg Box Publishing and Sean Purdy.

Editorial team:

Beatrice Armstrong
Krishan Coupland
Timothy Lawrence
Rachel Mendel
Matthew McGuinness
Faith Ng
Caroline Pearce
Lauren Rose
Naomi Spicer
Jo Surzyn
Laura Westerman

# Contents

Foreword
Steve Waters — *vii*

Contributors
Beatrice Armstrong
*Speed Dates* — *1*

Lauren Bishop
*Melissa's Bedroom* — *16*

David Burton
*Key Lime Pie* — *30*

Heather De Lyon
*Jasmine* — *46*

Cynthia Garcia
*Layla Gets a Treat* — *63*

UEA Anthology 2013

..........................................

Tim Lawrence
*Telling Tales* — 73

Gytha Lodge
*Dying for Darwin* — 81

Emma Maclusky
*The Waiter* — 92

Faith Ng
*Skin* — 97

Luke Wronski
*Vitamin G* — 105

..........................................

# Foreword

Steve Waters

Those who question the place of writing in Higher Education often imply that courses such as ours impose a kind of studied politeness on the unruly imaginations of their students; that writing, which as Sartre reminds us begins as an act of freedom, ends up as an act of duty; ends up, well, academic. The pages that follow give the lie to that particular canard. The writers therein are notable for their various points of origin across the globe, diverse in age, in ethnicity, in gender and probably sexuality (we don't inquire). But most importantly of all they are diverse in their vision of dramatic writing.

From a course that dares to think of drama in the round, this means they range across media: the students are encouraged to ask if their stories are best suited for the ear, the eye, the stage, the screen, indeed are invited to channel-hop between all these modes. Few writers in these times doggedly drill down into one medium alone, loftily indifferent to others.

But that's not the only diversity I mean; these writers 'contain multitudes' as Walt Whitman has it. After all the screenwriter excited by Michael Haneke is not always separable from the writer seeking to land a returning series for ITV1; the playwright conceiving of their work as a kind of painful confession, jostles against the audio writer whose imagination is kindled by distance and difference; the formalist contends with the omnivore of form, the stern classicist with the incontinent romantic. Sometimes these fights play out all in the same head, even in the same script, the kinds of struggle that might just generate *The Winter's Tale* for instance or maybe *The*

*Singing Detective*. Putting writers in a strongbox is not the task. (Having said that I can't resist a bit of writer-taxonomy. Alan Plater once said there were two sorts of writer: one who says, 'Look at me' and one who says 'Look at that'. I would finesse that further and add a third: the one who says, 'Look at me looking at that'.)

No, what a course like this can and should do is to release all the different possible writers our students bear within them. Having the courage to do that is what we should be evaluated on; the following pages attest to that aim at the least.

..................................................

Steve Waters, Tutor on MA Scriptwriting (and playwright, and sometime radio dramatist and very occasionally screenwriter).

# Beatrice Armstrong

Speed Dates
*Extract for stage*

### DATE NIGHT:

*1 sits facing the audience, as if on a date with them. The recorded VOICE that 1 converses with is played from behind or if possible from amongst the audience.*

**1:** So.
　　　Here we are then.

**VOICE:** Yes.

**1:** You look ... you look ... you look really ... well.

**VOICE:** Oh.
　　　　Thanks.
　　　　So do you.

**1:** That's what I thought.
　　　When I saw your picture.

**VOICE:** That's what you thought?

**1:** Yeah.
　　　I mean, no.
　　　No, of course not.

|        | Not that I don't think that you look well but … I thought you looked nice.
Attractive.
You look attractive now. |
|---|---|
| **VOICE:** | Thanks. So do you.
In a different way.
You know. |
| **1:** | Yeah.
Thanks.
I'm nervous. |
| **VOICE:** | Me too. I'm so, so nervous. |
| **1:** | Why? |
| **VOICE:** | Oh, I don't know. I haven't done this much. |
| **1:** | I can imagine. |
| **VOICE:** | What? |
| **1:** | I mean, you're … I'm sure that you could get someone easily without … you know. Just in a normal way. |
| **VOICE:** | Well, I'm busy, I guess.
Everyone is busy, these days.
This is the norm now, isn't it? It's not just for weirdos anymore! |
| **1:** | Oh yeah, me too, me too. |

VOICE: Have you done this? Before? Much?

1: A couple of times, yeah.

VOICE: How did it go?

1: Well. Yeah.

VOICE: It went well?

1: No.
It was fucking awful.

VOICE: Oh.
How come?

1: Well, the first time that I met someone, they looked nothing like their picture. Like, maybe that picture had been taken, like, four years ago or something and they'd had a lot of … well, kind of put on a lot of … life had not been kind, I suppose.
So I never called or anything. Not that I'm shallow, but it is dishonest.
And I hate dishonesty.
I actually hate it.
So that's why I never called.
Not just because of the … The second one was just … there wasn't any chemistry.

VOICE: Oh?

1: When we spoke online it was great, lots of banter.
'Got a live one!' That's what I thought.
But, well, no. No, not really. Not so much with the chemistry. You know?

**VOICE:** Yeah. Sure.

**1:** Yeah. And you?

**VOICE:** What?

**1:** How were your dates?

**VOICE:** Kind of the same.
One of them looked liked Tony Blair.
Something in the face.
Hard to explain.
It wasn't a good time to be looking like Tony Blair.
I mean, is there ever a good time for that? Was there ever a good time?
One of them was … well … kind of scary.

**1:** Oh no.

**VOICE:** I know. A definite killer's eyes.

**1:** Terrible.

**VOICE:** Yeah.

You can't always tell that, from a photograph.
Killer eyes.
They don't stand out for you in the same way that they do in the flesh.

**1:** No. I guess not. Or else nobody would end up …

**VOICE:** What?

**1:** Nothing.

**VOICE:** What, getting killed on a date?

**1:** Err, yeah.

**VOICE:** That doesn't happen.
Does that happen?

**1:** I don't know.
No.

**VOICE:** Of course not.

God, it could happen, couldn't it?
It actually could.

I mean, I'm always worried about kidneys, about baths full of ice. When you start to see someone, you let them buy you drinks and take you to places that you haven't been to before and that none of your friends have ever been to.

But then I watched this documentary about organ harvesting and apparently,
apparently
it doesn't really happen here.
But killing does, doesn't it? All the bloody time.

God.

Everything is so ... sorry.

**1:** No, no. I mean you're right ... everything is so ...
Anyway.
So,
anyway.

**VOICE:** Look, I don't ... I don't think this is gonna work.

**1:** Oh.
Right.
I'm sorry, but you brought it up.
The killer stuff.
And the kidney stuff.
That was you.

**VOICE:** I should go.

## Do you even have a face anymore?

*A lays in bed typing on a laptop, speaking aloud while typing. The replies are projected onto the back of the stage. The position of the bed should allow A to gaze out into the audience while waiting for the responses.*

**A:** I love you.

***Projection:*** *☺ xxxxxx*

**A:** God, I really, actually, totally love you.

***Projection:*** *LOL*
*Hyperlink*
*Picture of a kitten.*

**A:** I love your body.

***Projection:*** *;) ;) ;)*

**A:** And your essence.

***Projection:*** *!!!!!*

**A:** And your clothes.

***Projection:*** *ROFL.*

**A:** I wish that you were here.
It's really cold here and I just ...

I just wish that you were actually here.

***Projection:*** ☹☹☹

**A:** No, no, I'm not being needy or anything.
It would just be nice.

Nice to see you.

***Projection:*** *Hyperlink.*
*Picture of a puppy.*

**A:** Honestly, do I actually have a face anymore?

***Projection:*** ...

**A:** Do you actually even have a face anymore?
I mean, really?

***Projection:*** ... ☺ ?

**A:** That's sweet.

***Projection:*** *xxxx*

**A:** That's sweet.

***Projection:*** *xx.*

**A:**     Sweet.

I had this dream recently.

I woke up in a cold sweat.
I woke up choking.

All of my teeth fell out.
In the dream, I mean.
All of my teeth dropped straight out onto the table in front of me. *(A stops typing and just speaks.)* I was having dinner. They rattled one by one onto the plate that I was eating from; they sat in the gravy, in between some potatoes, in between some potatoes and all amongst some peas.

It didn't hurt me. I was horrified and I wanted to cry but my eyes felt stretched too wide for tears.
I wanted to cry but it didn't hurt me.
No pain.
No blood.
Just the clinking of the teeth hitting wood and china.

And nobody said anything. A whole restaurant full of people and not a word said about my plate full of teeth.

It's not that they didn't notice; I felt very sure at the time that people definitely did notice. It's just that they said nothing.
When I woke up, I lay on my own and that's what really troubled me; it troubled me then and it troubled me for the rest of the day: why didn't they say anything? They saw and they said nothing. And

then, as the day went on I wondered, would I have said anything? Would I be able to say something, if something like that happened in front of me?

Or if I was happy, even? Would I be able to say that out loud, to anyone? With their eyes and their head, right there in front of me?

Actual eyes.

I don't know.
I don't know.

I don't feel well.
I don't feel well.

I wish that you were here.
I wish that somebody was here.
You.
You, in particular. *(A starts typing again.)* You.

*Projection:*        …….

**A:**        Hey.
Look at this:
A frog sat like a human.
It's genius.
It's sat like a human.

But it isn't human.
It isn't human at all.

*Projection:*        *LOLS.*

## DATE NIGHT 2:

*2 sits facing the audience, as if on a date with them. The recorded VOICE that 2 converses with is played from behind or if possible from amongst the audience.*

**VOICE:** So. Here we are then.

**2:** So it seems.

**VOICE:** You look ... you look ... you look really ... well.

**2:** Is that a problem?

**VOICE:** That's what I thought. When I saw your picture.

**2:** Are you afraid of diseases?
Like, pathologically?
Are you saying that I look sick?
That I didn't look sick in my picture but now, bang, a sicko?

**VOICE:** Yeah. I mean, no.
No, of course not.
Not that I don't think that you look well but ... I thought you looked nice.
Attractive.
You look attractive now.

**2:** Well,
I'm not.
I'm not sick.

I don't know that I'm attractive either, really. I mean, nobody has ever said that to me.

|  |  |
|---|---|
|  | What, you actually think I'm attractive? That's ... well. I suppose that's nice. I suppose that I'm meant to want to be attractive. It's nice of you to say so. |
| VOICE: | Yeah. Thanks. I'm nervous. |
| 2: | Do you have an anxiety problem? Because that I could do without. |
| VOICE: | Why? |
| 2: | Seriously? I know it's hip but, actually, I have never found anxiety to be that sexy. It's not a freedom. That is such shit. I mean, I'm quite anxious. I'm a fairly anxious person. I've missed out on lots of things through anxiety. So I don't want to date someone with an anxiety problem. I've worked very hard not to have that kind of a problem. So I don't want to wake up next to one. |
| VOICE: | I can imagine. |
| 2: | Not that I'm cold or anything. I'm actually a very warm person. I think that comes across in my profile. Not that I wrote it myself; I'm not a narcissist. But I am warm. I'm a nice person to be around. |

**VOICE:** I mean you're ... I'm sure that you could get someone easily enough without ... you know. Just in a normal way.

**2:** Actually, I think most people are a bit underwhelming.

**VOICE:** Oh yeah, me too. Me too.

**2:** Dull.
I feel forced to shake things up. And I really don't like the feeling of feeling obliged.

Have you ever actually just screamed in someone's face?

**VOICE:** A couple of times, yeah.

**2:** Jesus.
I didn't see that one coming.

**VOICE:** Well. Yeah.

**2:** That's pretty fucked up.
It must have felt amazing.

**VOICE:** No. It was fucking awful.

**2:** On dates?
Did you scream on dates?
I bet you screamed on dates.
Or I bet you wanted to.
Why?

**VOICE:** Well, the first time that I met someone, they looked

nothing like their picture. Like, maybe that picture had been taken, like, four years ago or something and they'd had a lot of ... we'll, kind of put on a lot of ... life had not been kind, I suppose.
So I never called or anything. Not that I'm shallow, but it *is* dishonest.
And I hate dishonesty.
I actually hate it.
So that's why I never called.
Not just because of the ... The second one was just ... there wasn't any chemistry.

**2:** And that warrants screaming in someone's face, yeah?

**VOICE:** When we spoke online it was great, lots of banter. 'Got a live one!' That's what I thought.
But, well, no. No, not really. Not so much with the chemistry.
You know?

**2:** Not really.

**VOICE:** Yeah. And you?

**2:** I have never screamed in someone's face.
Not in a house.
Not in a supermarket.
Definitely not on a date.

**VOICE:** How were your dates?

**2:** I haven't done this kind of dating before.
I've been press-ganged into it.
My friend, Eliza; she made me a profile.

VOICE: Oh no.

2: Yeah.
She's a pushy bastard.

VOICE: Terrible.

2: I wouldn't even be here if I didn't think she'd never shut up if I didn't try.

I mean, I was surprised, when I saw your message.
You looked really hot.
In that photograph.

VOICE: Yeah.

2: Ultimately though, I was pissed. I was pissed at being made to take part in the whole online thing.
I mean, fuck off Eliza.
If I want to die alone, I'll die alone, OK?
I mean is it reasonable that I am subjected to this kind of pressure?
Is this a thing?
Is this how we live now?

VOICE: No. I guess not. Or else nobody would end up …

2: Dying alone? Achieving nothing?

VOICE: Nothing.

2: So.
I dunno.
I mean, should we fuck?

VOICE: Errr, yeah?

2:      Wow.
        The passion.
        How do you like to fuck?

**VOICE:** I don't know.

2:      So I'm guessing you didn't get into this just to fuck, then?

**VOICE:** Of course not.

2:      Well.
        I think this is pretty much done now, right?
        I don't massively fancy you and if we aren't going to fuck, I have stuff to do.

**VOICE:** No.
        No.
        I mean you're right, everything is so …
        Anyway.
        So,
        anyway.

2:      God.
        Fucking hell.
        You should see somebody.
        About your anxiety problems.
        It's kind of gross, actually.

1:      Oh.
        Right.

...........................................................

Beatrice Armstrong is interested in writing for theatre and for radio. She was selected by theatre audiences to be a finalist in 2011's Offcut Festival for her short piece *Alternative Therapy*. Her first full-length stage play *Battery* was produced by fEast Theatre Company in 2012.

# Lauren Bishop

Melissa's Bedroom
*Short film script*

INT. MELISSA'S BEDROOM

A small, cluttered bedroom with laundry strewn over almost every surface. Promotional posters, playbills and tickets have been tacked, seemingly at random, along the walls and on the corkboard behind the desk. Fairy lights dangle, crooked, over the drawn curtains. Two full bottles of store-brand vodka sit discreetly under the desk. A stuffed lion toy sits on a chair in the corner.

A folded and frayed photo is taped to the back of the bedroom door.

INSERT: PHOTOGRAPH

A beaming BLONDE GIRL, no older than seven, wearing a fairy costume. Her mother stands over her, blonde and radiant, kissing the top of her head. Her father, MATTHEW, who is dark-haired and in his 30s, has his arm slung around her shoulders and a playbill in his hand for *A Midsummer Night's Dream*. A childish autograph is scrawled over the front.

BACK TO SCENE

MELISSA, 17, sits on the bed with her laptop on her knees, typing and listening to music. Her hair has been dyed bright red, but she is clearly the same girl. She's dressed for cold weather, layers, scarf and all. Someone taps at the door hesitantly. There is a pause before they knock a little harder.

                **MELISSA**
                (Loudly)
What?

The door opens and a head pokes in. ELLIE, 11, looks meek and entirely out of place in Melissa's bedroom. She's still wearing her school uniform.

                **ELLIE**
          Dad said it's almost time for
          dinner.

                **MELISSA**
I'm busy.

                **ELLIE**
Yeah, but Dad said to –

                **MELISSA**
          'Not take no for an answer', I
          know.

Ellie pushes the door open slightly and it knocks against a pile of clothes. She looks up apologetically, but Melissa is too distracted to notice.

                **ELLIE**
What're you working on?

                **MELISSA**
Stuff for class.

**ELLIE**
Is it hard?
(Glimmer of pride)
I had to write two sides the other day.
(Deflated)
I bet yours is harder though.

**MELISSA**
Yeah.

**ELLIE**
What's it about?

Ellie steps inside and quietly shuts the door behind her. Melissa still hasn't noticed.

**MELISSA**
Stuff. Chemistry. Maths. Biology.
Whatever you're least interested in, Els.

**ELLIE**
Maths isn't too bad, actually –

**MELISSA**
Then I'm doing chemistry.

**ELLIE**
Oh.

Ellie moves towards the bed as if she's approaching a wild animal.

**ELLIE**
Lissa?

(Beat)
Um, Mum's worried about you.

Melissa looks up reproachfully. Ellie almost jumps, but manages to correct herself.

**ELLIE**
I mean, Sarah. Sarah's worried.
Like you're sick or something.
You don't seem sick, though.

**MELISSA**
I'm not sick.

**ELLIE**
Well yeah, I know that, I just heard her talking to Dad and thought I should tell you.

**MELISSA**
(With an edge)
What'd she say?

Ellie chews on the inside of her lip. She's beginning to regret bringing it up in the first place.

**ELLIE**
(Uneasily)
I dunno – a bunch of stuff.

**MELISSA**
Like?

**ELLIE**
Like ... You're always busy, and how you shout a lot and sleep all the time and keep skipping dinner. And you stopped spending time with your friends and stuff. And you exercise too much.

Melissa scowls.

**ELLIE**
She thinks you're getting too thin.

Something flashes over Melissa's face and Ellie backpedals instinctively.

**ELLIE**
I mean, I don't think you are, I think you look totally normal. And if you were really thin, wouldn't you be showing it off, or something?

Melissa stares at her, but Ellie can't stop herself.

**ELLIE**
Like, you've always got those big hoodies on and –
(Beat)
– erm – well, that's what she said.

Melissa sets her laptop to the side, swinging her legs over the edge of the bed in one angry movement to face her.

**MELISSA**
You know what? If they have some sort of problem, they can come up here and say it to my face, not whisper behind my back like children. If they're going to tell me to act like a bloody adult all the time, they should stop bitching about me when I can't read their fucking minds and figure out what they're angry about this time. I deal with enough of that shit at college!

Ellie stares at her, rooted to the spot. She bites down hard on her lip.

**MELISSA**
So when they ask why I'm not coming to dinner, tell them that.

**ELLIE**
(Quietly)
But Dad said –

**MELISSA**
I don't care what Dad said. Dad can piss off. I'm having a shower.

Melissa turns away and starts to unknot her scarf, tossing it onto the floor with unnecessary force. She yanks down the zip of her hoodie and gives Ellie a stern look over her shoulder.

Ellie doesn't budge, but her lip is quivering. She catches a glimpse of Melissa's protruding collarbone. Her eyes widen slightly.

**ELLIE**
Lissa?

**MELISSA**
Go. Away.

**ELLIE**
But –

**MELISSA**
Get out!

She takes two firm steps towards Ellie, who recoils and heads for the door. She slams it shut behind her.

Ellie's quick footsteps fade out of earshot as Melissa stares at the door. She takes a shuddering breath and continues to undress.

**FLASHFORWARD TO:**

**INT. MELISSA'S BEDROOM – DAY**

The doorknob turns softly, and a tall, slightly heavy-set man steps inside with a small suitcase. MATTHEW is 42 now, and it looks as though domestic life has softened him since the photograph on the door was taken. He carries guilt on his shoulders like a cloak.

He switches the light on.

The bedroom looks much like it did before, but the clothes are scattered in different places on the floor. Glossy *Vogue* and *Glamour* magazines are similarly spread out across the room. Dozens of magazine pages, all of which feature waifish models, have been pinned up on the corkboard that overlooks Melissa's desk. They cover the playbills and

tickets. Similar photos have been scattered over the walls.
Matthew sets the suitcase onto Melissa's bed and unzips it.

He gingerly steps around a pile of clothes to turn on the desk lamp. He fumbles for the iPhone in his pocket and swipes across the screen to unlock it.

He scrolls through his apps.

**INSERT: IPHONE**

The background image is a photo of his family in the mountains, with his arms slung around the shoulders of Ellie and a dark-haired woman, SARAH. Melissa is standing at a distance from her stepmother, staring sulkily into the camera.

**BACK TO SCENE**

Matthew taps on the voice memo application. Swallows. Presses the record button. Clears his throat.

**INSERT: IPHONE**

00:00 ticks to 00:01.

**BACK TO SCENE**

He lifts the iPhone to his mouth and speaks into it, turning in a slow circle as he takes the bedroom in and lingers on the magazine pages.

>                    **MATTHEW**
> Lissa. I, uh, wanted to record this to
> explain. Well, there isn't really much
> to explain, but, erm. You know.

**FLASHFORWARD BEGINS:**

**EXT. STREET – AFTERNOON**

Matthew places the suitcase into the boot of a small Nissan. It's winter, and the sky is getting dark already. A totally stripped Christmas tree sits next to the bins, waiting for collection.

His breath puffs out in front of him.

> **MATTHEW (VO)**
> By now, you've probably settled in at the clinic in Southampton. And we probably had a fight in the car on the way there. You might feel betrayed. Angry. And I understand that.

His hands shake as he slams the door shut with more force than necessary.

**FLASHFORWARD ENDS**

**INT. MELISSA'S BEDROOM – DAY**

Those same shaking hands push in the chair at Melissa's desk and fluff the pillow.

> **MATTHEW (VO)**
> I – well, I'm doing this because I don't know if you're going to listen to me much when I pick you up from college and tell you where I'm taking you.

He unplugs the laptop from its cord and sets it carefully in the suitcase.

## FLASHFORWARD BEGINS:

### INT./EXT. MATTHEW'S NISSAN/STREET – AFTERNOON

Matthew is driving silently, face ashen. His hands are clasped tight around the steering wheel. He's on autopilot.

### INSERT: DASHBOARD CLOCK

It reads 16:26.

### BACK TO SCENE

> **MATTHEW (VO)**
> But whatever you say to me, and however angry you get –

He mouths along with the next few words, as if he can hear the recording echoing in his head.

> **MATTHEW (VO)**
> I still love you. You know that, but I just want to say it again.
> 'Cos I do.

He flicks on his turning signal.

Westonborough College looms in the distance as STUDENTS begin to trickle out of the building in groups.

                MATTHEW (VO)
        And I wish we didn't have to do
        this. I wish that you weren't –

Matthew's voice in the recording falters and trails off as he catches sight of his daughter.

Melissa trudges behind the mobs, stopping in Matthew's headlights and squinting into the car. Her coat, scarf and hat dwarf her entirely. The bright light makes her look sickly.

                MATTHEW (VO)
                (Quietly)
        I wouldn't do this if you weren't ill.

                **FLASHFORWARD ENDS**

Matthew traces the laptop's cord under the desk, and his eyes fall on two empty bottles of store-brand vodka and a crumpled box of diet pills. His breath catches.

                MATTHEW (VO)
        I wouldn't do this if I didn't have
        to.

                **FLASHFORWARD BEGINS:**

**INT./EXT. MATTHEW'S NISSAN/STREET – AFTERNOON**

TIGHT on Matthew as the passenger door opens and Melissa slides into the seat. He's breathing a little faster. His eyes bore holes into the windshield as he stares straight ahead.

> **MATTHEW (VO)**
> I know you'll be upset, but we can't just stand by and let you waste away. We can't. I can't.

Melissa's seatbelt buckle clicks. Her iPod blares a distant, droning beat.

> **MATTHEW (VO)**
> Lissa, you're my little girl. You're my first. I'm meant to protect you.

He runs a hand through his hair. Swallows. He hesitates for a moment before he automatically locks the doors.

**FLASHFORWARD ENDS**

**INT. MELISSA'S BEDROOM – DAY**

Matthew checks his watch –

**INSERT: WATCHFACE**

It reads 15:54.

**BACK TO SCENE**

He packs faster, still clutching his iPhone in one hand, still recording. He yanks open the drawer of her wardrobe, fumbling through unfolded shirts, pairs of jeans, jumpers, socks, underwear, bras.

> **MATTHEW**
> I wish I'd noticed sooner. I'm sorry I didn't notice sooner.

Clothes pile up in the open suitcase on her bed, all unfolded.

> **MATTHEW**
> You probably hate me for doing this, and that's fair enough. You probably feel furious and betrayed and, God, I would understand if you never spoke to me again. I would. Because I feel like I've betrayed you, but the appointments aren't working. And you keep dropping weight and I just don't –

He pulls out a handful of socks and stops, taking a shaky breath. A framed photograph sits at the bottom of the drawer.

**INSERT: PHOTOGRAPH**

Matthew holds back Melissa's hair as she blows out a large '12' candle on her birthday cake. Ellie, 7, wears a party hat and a goofy smile. Her front teeth are missing.

The blonde woman, her mother, is notably absent.

Matthew picks up the photograph and rubs his thumb along the edges of the frame, smudging it.

> **MATTHEW (VO)**
> ... I don't know if you'll ever bother to listen to this, Lissa.

**BACK TO SCENE**

He sets the framed photograph in the suitcase and turns to

search through the dirty laundry and scattered *Vogue* and *Glamour* magazines. Finally, he finds the tattered, stuffed lion and carefully places it in the suitcase.

He turns to the bookcase and completely avoids the stacks of magazines, tracing his hand along the shelf of DVDs, picking out three – *Beetlejuice, The Princess Bride, Amélie*. He packs them as well.

### INT./EXT. MATTHEW'S NISSAN/STREET – NIGHT

Matthew drives back in the dark, passenger seat empty.

> **MATTHEW**
> But I wish I'd been there for you
> the way I promised I would be,
> when she left. I love you, Lissa.
> I'll – I'll see you on the weekends.
> I swear.

He mouths the words to himself as he drives, and the long finished recording sees him off into the darkness.

### END

...........................................

Lauren Bishop has a particular interest in writing for British television, writing for children, and playing with genre. Her recent works include *The Flood Walls*, a feature-length noir piece, *The Station*, an animated television series, and *Bamarre*, a feature-length adaptation of Gail Carson Levine's *The Two Princesses of Bamarre*.

# David Burton

Key Lime Pie
*A short film script*

**INT. DINER – DAY**

Booths with wooden tables, each one with a small jukebox.

Scattered men in flannel shirts sip coffee, but no one is looking at a paper. This isn't the type of place where people read.

JACK MARLING, early 40s, sporting a utilitarian haircut and what might pass for a suit in the Midwest, is also sipping coffee, black. Across from him is ANTHONY DANOWITZ, late 40s, overdressed.

They sit in front of a window which overlooks the parking lot and lets in the sun. A Crown Victoria can be seen parked outside.

Jack slaps a briefcase onto the table.

                **JACK**
    This is it. Your new life.
    Everything. Birth certificate.
    High school diploma. A driver's
    license with your new name …

              **ANTHONY**
    My name?

### JACK (CONT'D)
Cecil Smalls.

### ANTHONY
Cecil Smalls? That sounds like a jerk. Why can't I pick the name?

### JACK
The department picks the name. You've got a part-time job in a lumber yard.

### ANTHONY
And what? I'm Cecil Smalls now and I'm a fucking lumber jockey?

### JACK
Part-time lumber jockey. In Templeton, Idaho. In this house.

Jack passes a photo across the table.

### ANTHONY
That house is a piece of shit.

### JACK
Then go back home to Manhattan after you testify. It would save the taxpayers a lot of money and grief. It's going to cost nearly seventy grand a year just to keep you breathing.

> ANTHONY
>
> That's more than your salary isn't it? Even your bosses think I'm worth more than you, and they think I'm a scumbag.
>
> JACK
>
> Look at that nice girl over there. Hard worker. Pretty.

Jack motions with his cup of coffee towards STARLA, late 20s with a mop of hair falling across her forehead. She's wiping down the counter.

> JACK (CONT'D)
>
> How do you think she'd like to know that when you die the roses on your casket will be paid for with her tax money?
>
> ANTHONY
>
> I bet you twenty bucks that she'd be happy about it.
>
> JACK
>
> Twenty bucks? That she'll be happy to pay for flowers at your funeral? Make it forty.

Anthony nods and drops a quarter into the jukebox. Procol Harum's *A Whiter Shade of Pale* swells.

He closes his eyes and takes it in.

**ANTHONY**
Ah, this one takes me back. 1979.

He taps a pack of cigarettes on the table and one falls out. He lights it and inhales.

**ANTHONY (CONT'D)**
I was down on the Coney Island boardwalk with Shelly Winkleman. And we were walking past the shills and the eggmen and the cons, and I never stop, right, because I know that they've got it all figured out. There's no way to beat them.

**JACK**
I'll bet you I can tell you where you got your shoes ...

**ANTHONY**
... You got them on your feet. Right. You know the drill. But for some reason, with this one guy, I stopped. He was standing there holding a shoebox. And maybe because I never seen this gag before, or maybe it was fate, I don't know, but I stopped. And he said 'I bet you ...'

STARLA appears at the table.

**STARLA**
What can I get y'all?

**JACK**

Mornin', I'll have the tomato soup. And an egg cream.

**STARLA**

And for you?

Anthony squints at her name badge.

**ANTHONY**

I don't know ... Starla. What won't make me sick?

**STARLA**

Everything but the egg cream. But if you want to know what the best thing is, I reckon it's our Key Lime Pie.

**ANTHONY**

You hear that? Starla reckons it's the Key Lime Pie. What do you reckon Jack?

**JACK**

I reckon you're an asshole.

**ANTHONY**

I'll have the tomato soup as well.

**STARLA**

I think really you oughta try the Key Lime Pie. If you're just passing through you might never have the chance again.

**ANTHONY**
What's with the fucking Key Lime Pie? I'll have the soup.

**STARLA**
It's just that I'll bet you ...

**ANTHONY**
You'll bet me? She'll bet me.

**STARLA**
I'll bet you it's the best pie that you've ever tasted.

**ANTHONY**
Yeah?

**JACK**
This is what he does. He bets.

**ANTHONY**
OK. If this is the best pie I've ever tasted then I'll leave this shitbox house to you when I die.

He slides the photo of the house across the table.

**ANTHONY (CONT'D)**
It's in Idaho. Probably some great bingo halls out there.

**STARLA**
You'll give me that house?

**ANTHONY**

Well, not until I die. And not the house itself. Jack here ...

Jack waves at Starla.

**JACK**

Hello again.

**ANTHONY**

Will liquidate the house and you'll receive the money. But then ... what's the house valued at Jack?

**JACK**

$178,000.

**ANTHONY**

Like I said, it's a shitbox. That $178,000 will be taken to the Golden Nugget in Reno. They have no limit roulette there. And you'll put it on red. Ever been to Reno?

**STARLA**

Pardon me?

**ANTHONY**

No, fuck it. You can choose, red or black. Control your own destiny, it's better that way. And *if* you win, the $356,000 is yours to keep. But only *if* this is the *best* pie I've ever had.

> **STARLA**
> I don't know what ...

> **ANTHONY**
> And it must be, because you told me it was, and you wouldn't lie.

> **STARLA**
> And suppose you don't agree that it's the best pie you've ever had?

> **ANTHONY**
> Then you dance with me, right here, to *A Whiter Shade of Pale*, because, goddamnit, I never got to dance with Shelly Winkleman to it, and that's what should have happened that night.

JACK just sits, drinking his coffee. He has no dog in this fight. He lights a cigarette.

> **ANTHONY (CONT'D)**
> Maybe things would have been different then.

> **STARLA**
> Right. I guess I better go and put a cherry on top. For luck.

Starla, nervous, turns to walk away.

> **JACK**
> And cancel the egg cream.

Anthony turns back to Jack.

**ANTHONY**

So anyway. '79. Coney Island Boardwalk. The shoebox. And this shill says to me, he says 'I'll bet you that I can show you and your lady the freakiest thing you've ever seen in your life.' And so I says, what's the bet? And he tells me it's $20 for him to show us, but if it's not the freakiest thing we've ever seen, he'll give us 50 back.

**JACK**

50 back? That's a good deal.

**ANTHONY**

It *is* a good deal, because I figure I'll just tell him some bullshit about some freakier thing I saw and he'll give us 50 and we'll walk away and have some cotton candy and get drunk at Cusomano's bar where they served underage kids ...but if that's what had happened, I wouldn't remember it.

**JACK**

You never get a good deal on the boardwalk.

**ANTHONY**
No. What happened is that he opened the box. We looked. And then we didn't ask for the 50. We walked away, and this song here, *A Whiter Shade of Pale*, started playing, and we went separate ways and never saw each other again. But because of that night, I am who I am today. Because of that night I'm being forced to become a part-time lumber jockey called Cecil Smalls and live in what was probably a confiscated meth lab. You know that shit is toxic. It sticks to the walls, right?

**JACK**
It isn't a confiscated meth lab. What was in the box?

**ANTHONY**
You don't wanna know, Jack.

**JACK**
I do. What was in the box?

Anthony takes a long drag from his cigarette and smashes it out.

**ANTHONY**
A tiny man.

**JACK**
Get the fuck outta here.

**ANTHONY**
No, I'm being serious. Look me in the eyes and tell me I'm lying.

Jack stares at him for a few seconds and then smashes his cigarette out too.

**ANTHONY (CONT'D)**
And not a baby neither. I mean, a tiny black *man*. In a shoebox. And he looked like he was trying to talk but he couldn't form the words. He just turned his head and looked at me and it looked like he was gonna cry. And then the man closed the box.

**JACK**
And now you're giving away houses in diners.

**ANTHONY**
Now I'm giving away houses in diners because after that, shit doesn't make sense. The world doesn't make sense. There are tiny men you never hear about kept in boxes on the beach and there's shit a lot crazier than that out there, believe it. You buy your shitty suits at Men's Warehouse and spend your life lugging briefcases like that one into shitty diners like this one and putting guys like me into falling down houses

in places like Idaho and act like you're saving the world, and it doesn't mean anything. We're living in somebody's fucking dream. Morality is relative.

### JACK

I live in this world, buddy. I don't know what the fuck place you're living in, but I don't want to visit.

### ANTHONY

So, now the waitress is going to think differently. Bigger. Whether she wins the bet or not, and then whether she wins on roulette or not, is irrelevant. Because now she's thinking about having $356,000, which she never could have imagined before she came into work this morning. And when you get used to expecting that kind of money, then suddenly $2.50 an hour plus tips doesn't cut it anymore.

### JACK

So now she's going to be unfulfilled in her work.

### ANTHONY

Yes! Yes. But she already was. It's just that now she's gonna start to take risks. Now she's gonna have a successful mindset.

**JACK**
This is the most fucked up breakfast I've ever had. Can't we just talk about baseball?

Starla arrives at the table, carrying a tray.

**STARLA**
Order up for the high rollers.

**ANTHONY**
Got a pen, Starla?

Starla pulls a pen from her apron and passes it to Anthony, who's smoothing out his paper place mat.

**ANTHONY (CONT'D)**
All right, this here is a binding will that recognizes Starla ...

**STARLA**
Cranford.

**ANTHONY**
Starla Cranford as my beneficiary. Upon my unfortunate death, many, many years from now, my house is to be liquidated and the assets left to Starla Cranford in the form of a marker at the Golden Nugget Casino. There's only one thing I'd like to ask, if it's not too much trouble darling.

**STARLA**
What's that?

**ANTHONY**
Would you be kind enough to buy some yellow roses for my casket?

**STARLA**
Yeah. Of course.

Anthony looks over at Jack. Jack opens his wallet and takes out two $20 bills. He tosses them over towards Anthony.

**JACK**
Un-fucking-believable.

**ANTHONY**
But of course, of course this is all conditional on whether or not Starla is telling the truth. If this is not the best piece of pie I've ever tasted, then she's gonna dance with me right here. Like it's 1979. Coney Island.

**STARLA**
I don't know what that means.

**JACK**
You don't want to.

Jack takes a spoonful of his soup and looks out the window. A truck is attaching the Crown Vic to a winch.

**JACK**
Ah, shit.

**EXT. DINER PARKING LOT – DAY**

Jack runs towards the car.

> **JACK**
> Hey, hey. I'm right here.
>
> **TOWTRUCK OPERATOR**
> You were parked in a handicapped spot.
>
> **JACK**
> I'll move it, I'll move it. I didn't see a sign. Let me just move it.
>
> **TOWTRUCK OPERATOR**
> It's already on the winch now so I can't …
>
> **JACK**
> Look around, there's no one else here. There's no handicapped person who needs that spot.
>
> **TOWTRUCK OPERATOR**
> Sorry. Like I said, now that I've got it hooked …
>
> **JACK**
> Ah, this is a fucked up world.

Through the door, the notes of *A Whiter Shade of Pale* drift out.

**INT. DINER – DAY**

> **JACK**
> What? He already tried it?

Anthony is sprawled on the floor. He's not moving. Starla is panicky.

**STARLA**
We ... we were dancing and he started choking. On the cherry. For luck.

Jack reaches down and feels for a pulse. Nothing.

**JACK**
Just now, maybe you couldn't hear him, but when I bent down just now, he said 'that was the best pie I ever had.'

**STARLA**
Really? Are you sure?

**JACK**
I would bet on it.

Through the window, Jack's car is towed away.

**END**

........................................................

David Burton grew up in Connecticut and studied English at Elmira College. He's worked as a record company scout, a storm chaser, a professional gambler, and an inventor of cocktails. He lives in Norwich with his wife and daughter, and is currently working on his third feature screenplay.

# Heather De Lyon

Jasmine

**INT. SITTING ROOM, CARL AND SHERYLL'S FLAT – NIGHT**

A small, basic modern flat. CARL (20), good-looking, wearing jeans and T-shirt, is lying across the cheap, bright sofa. JASMINE (3) is asleep next to him, wearing pyjamas and rabbit slippers. Plastic toddler toys are strewn round the room. SHERYLL (19), pretty, a little overweight, long black hair, and slightly too much make-up, tidies toys into a box.

          **SHERYLL**
        Tracey's gutted. You better not do
        that to me Carl or I'll kill you.

          **CARL**
        Why would I, babes? When I got
        you and my little princess.

CARL ruffles JASMINE's hair. She stirs and turns over, but stays asleep.

          **SHERYLL**
        Don't wake her, stupid. Put the
        DVD on.

**CARL**
Don't know why Darren went out with her in the first place. What DVD we watching?

**SHERYLL**
Tracey's a good mate.

**CARL**
She's a selfish cow.

**SHERYLL**
*Vampire Diaries* OK?

**CARL**
You better watch out. Now Darren's ditched her she'll be totally jealous of us. She knows how to stir it up, Tracey does.

**INT. CARL AND SHERYLL'S SITTING ROOM – DAY**

JASMINE, humming, wearing rabbit slippers and jeans under a pink fake fur coat, is jumping around on the sofa.

SHERYLL, getting fraught, tries to do up JASMINE's coat buttons.

**SHERYLL**
Stay still. Let me do it up for you.

SHERYLL manages two buttons. A shower is running nearby. SHERYLL shouts.

**SHERYLL**
Come on Carl. You're using all the hot water.

SHERYLL wrestles JASMINE's feet into shoes. SHERYLL is exasperated. CARL comes in, towelling his hair.

CARL leans over SHERYLL, her head bent over JASMINE. He lifts her hair, kissing the back of her neck.

CARL shakes drips over them. JASMINE shrieks with delight.

**JASMINE**
Daddy's raining on me, Mummy.

They clown around giggling. CARL holds SHERYLL in a close embrace, kissing her nose.

**CARL**
All this we got. May not've been how we planned, but I wouldn't change a thing. Remember that babes. Promise?

SHERYLL steps back, pulls her stomach in and smoothes down her top.

**SHERYLL**
Promise.

SHERYLL glances in the mirror, turns sideways, smoothing her top and breathing her stomach in again.

**CARL**
We better go babes or we'll miss the start. We going to the cinema, Jasmine?

**SHERYLL**
Be exciting won't it, sweetheart?

### EXT. CINEMA COMPLEX – DAY

CARL, SHERYLL and JASMINE, in her buggy, leave the cinema, smiling happily, with TRACEY (20), dyed blonde hair, and too-short skirt.

**TRACEY**
You're lucky to have Sheryll. Hope you know that Carl. Doin' your share with Jasmine?

### INT. CARL AND SHERYLL'S SITTING ROOM – DAY

SHERYLL hums happily, putting breakfast things away. JASMINE sits on the floor rolling a ball against the skirting board.

**JASMINE**
One, two, nine. Mummy play.

**SHERYLL**
In a minute.

SHERYLL sings. A mobile on the worktop buzzes. SHERYLL glances at it. The sender's name flashes up – 'CHANTAL'. SHERYLL picks up the mobile, checks the message, which reads, 'Starbucks at 12? xx'. SHERYLL freezes.

CARL hurries into the room, in manual work overalls, grabs his phone (that SHERYLL has been looking at) and kisses her.

                    **CARL**
            Bye babes. Won't be late.

CARL doesn't notice SHERYLL's mood change. He leaves.

                    **JASMINE**
            Mummy. Mummy play. Three, five.

JASMINE continues rolling the ball. It thumps repeatedly against the skirting board. SHERYLL snaps.

                    **SHERYLL**
            Stop that Jasmine. You're giving me a headache.

SHERYLL takes the ball from JASMINE who starts whimpering. SHERYLL picks up her mobile.

                    **SHERYLL (CONT'D)**
            Hi Mum. You busy today? (pause)
            OK. No problem. Love you too.


**EXT. STARBUCKS – DAY**

SHERYLL, grim-faced, pushes JASMINE past shops and eateries. The Starbucks sign is up ahead, on the opposite side of the road.

SHERYLL hesitates as she approaches Starbucks.
CARL sits at a window-table, next to an attractive girl, CHANTAL, (21) with long blonde hair. CARL has his arm round her shoulder. She has her face in her hands and leans on his shoulder.
SHERYLL stops abruptly, turns and heads away, pushing the buggy crazily past other pedestrians. SHERYLL wipes tears off her face, eye make-up smearing.

### EXT. STARK MODERN BLOCK OF FLATS – DAY

SHERYLL piles plastic sacks and toddler paraphernalia into an old red Corsa. CARL pulls up on a moped.

**CARL**
What the hell's going on?

**SHERYLL**
Get out my way.

**CARL**
Sheryll. What you doing?

**SHERYLL**
I got nothin' to say to you Carl.

**CARL**
Is this that cow Tracey stirring it?

**SHERYLL**
You promised me.

**CARL**
She's not doin' you any favours, Sheryll, cos, God's truth, I ain't done nothin'.

**SHERYLL**
Why'd she make stuff up?

**CARL**
You know why.

SHERYLL wavers. JASMINE begins crying. CARL leans down to undo her buggy strap.

**SHERYLL**
Leave her Carl. Mummy'll only be a minute, sweetheart.

SHERYLL piles the last bags into the boot.

**CARL**
Don't cry princess. Here. What's Daddy got?

CARL carries her to his moped, takes an Asda carrier bag off the handlebars. He takes out a sticky lolly and a banana.

JASMINE takes both – one in each hand. CARL smiles.

**CARL (CONT'D)**
Good girl. Yeah. You eat your five a day. Make you a good swimmer like your mum and dad.

SHERYLL takes JASMINE, stuffing her into the car seat. As SHERYLL does this, CARL opens the boot and takes out a plastic bin-bag.

> **SHERYLL**
> Stop being childish, Carl.

> **CARL**
> At least talk to me.

The bag splits, tumbling toys onto the pavement. SHERYLL scrabbles round stuffing toys back in the plastic bin-bag.

CARL looks down at SHERYLL. JASMINE is crying. He takes SHERYLL's hand. A moped pulls up next to them. One of CARL's friends, JAKE, jumps off.

> **JAKE**
> Hi Sheryll. Wotcha mate. How's Chantal doing now?

SHERYLL pulls her hand out of CARL's, shoves the bin-bag into the car, slams the door and drives off.

**EXT. SHERYLL'S MOTHER'S HOUSE – DAY**

CARL hammers the front door of a bleak-looking house on a run-down estate. SHERYLL's MOTHER, IRENE (41), opens the upstairs window.

> **IRENE**
> You can piss right off, Carl. You done enough damage.

> **CARL**
> I just wanna see them.

#### IRENE
You should've thought of that sooner.

#### CARL
What's that mean?

#### IRENE
You should've kept it in your trousers.

#### CARL
What the fuck you talking about?

#### IRENE
Sheryll's told us what you done. Don't think you gonna see Jasmine any time soon.

#### CARL
Where is she?

#### IRENE
Think I'd tell you that?

#### CARL
I got a right to see my daughter.

#### IRENE
Shit like you got no rights.

IRENE slams the window shut.

### INT./EXT. SHOPPING PRECINCT – DAY

CARL walks along, shoulders hunched, smoking. He sees SHERYLL, with JASMINE in a buggy.

**CARL**
(shouting) Sheryll! Jasmine!

CARL runs over to them, stubs out the cigarette, squats down by his daughter.

**CARL**
Hallo. How's my little princess?

**SHERYLL**
Leave her alone, Carl.

SHERYLL pushes CARL, unbalances him and moves away, weaving between shoppers. CARL picks himself up and runs after her.

**CARL**
Stop. Sheryll. Give me a chance.
You got it wrong.

**SHERYLL**
Leave us alone.

**CARL**
I never done nothin'.

**SHERYLL**
Why should I believe you?

**CARL**
Cos it's true.

SHERYLL hesitates, uncertain, then walks into Poundland. CARL follows.

**CARL**
Won't you even let me explain?

**SHERYLL**
What's to explain, Carl? I got eyes. You and that moo Chantal.

**CARL**
Wasn't what it looked like Sheryll. She just heard her twin sister lost the baby.

**SHERYLL**
What baby? I don't know nothin' 'bout no baby.

**CARL**
I'm tryin' to tell you, if you'd fuckin' listen.

**SHERYLL**
I'm busy Carl. I gotta get stuff.

**CARL**
I'll look after her. You get your shopping. We'll stay here.

CARL squats by JASMINE. SHERYLL looks harassed, like any

mother with too much to do. She accepts CARL's offer, leaving JASMINE with CARL.

When SHERYLL has gone, CARL pushes the buggy out of the shop. JASMINE smiles. He moves swiftly but without drawing attention. We can't see SHERYLL, who shouts.

        **SHERYLL**
        Where are you? Don't do this to me. Jasmine! Jasmine!

CARL weaves between shoppers, trying to stay hidden from SHERYLL.

        **SHERYLL**
        You're being an idiot, Carl. You won't get away with this.

CARL gets caught in a group of shoppers and can't get through. SHERYLL catches up and tries to grab the buggy, pushing CARL out of the way.

A SECURITY GUARD runs over, placing a firm hand on CARL's arm. CARL tries to shake him off but, in the distraction, SHERYLL grabs the buggy and hurries away.

        **SECURITY GUARD**
        Better let go of that, son. Don't want any trouble do we?

CARL shakes off the SECURITY GUARD.

        **CARL**
        Get off me. That's my daughter. I can see my daughter, can't I?

CARL shakes himself free, strides off, seeing SHERYLL ahead. He runs to catch her. SHERYLL turns and sees him following, just as she reaches the exit.

SHERYLL runs out of the precinct, looking back, not concentrating on where she is going.

She runs into the road, slamming into the side of a passing car. There's a screech of brakes, a scream and crunch of a buggy wheel. The buggy whirls out of control. SHERYLL is knocked into the road where she lies slumped and still.

The buggy ricochets off the car and back onto the pavement, glancing a concrete pillar, then caught by a passer-by.

### INT. HOSPITAL BED – DAY

CARL walks into a hospital room. He looks at SHERYLL, who lies, eyes closed, hooked up to machines. SHERYLL's MOTHER, IRENE, sits next to her. CARL holds a bunch of supermarket carnations awkwardly in one hand and a balloon. Machines beep.

              **CARL**
Hallo.

              **IRENE**
Let you in then, did they?

CARL stands awkwardly staring at SHERYLL.

           **IRENE (CONT'D)**
What riff-raff you got looking after my granddaughter?

A NURSE bustles in.

                **NURSE**
        I'm afraid we don't allow flowers.
        (pause) The balloon's fine.

                **CARL**
        Sorry.

The NURSE checks machines. CARL carefully ties the balloon-string round the bed-end.

## INT. SWIMMING POOL – DAY

JASMINE and CARL are in the swimming pool playing. JASMINE splashes around in toddler armbands.

                **CARL**
        You're my little mermaid. You a mermaid, Jasmine? You got a fishy's tail?

                **JASMINE**
        No Daddy. Me not a fishy.

JASMINE giggles, splashing, then goes still and serious.

                **JASMINE**
        When Mummy coming? When Mummy home?

                **CARL**
        Soon princess. Mummy be better soon.

> JASMINE
>
> Mummy in hospital.

> CARL
>
> Yeah, but soon be fixed.

A ball bounces near them, breaking the tension, distracting JASMINE, who pushes it away, giggling.

**INT. CARL'S FLAT, SITTING-ROOM – DAY**

CARL and JASMINE sit together on the settee. JASMINE, wearing the same rabbit slippers, pats a Staffordshire terrier puppy sitting beside her.

> CARL
>
> Be nice to Buddy. Gently.

> JASMINE
>
> Mummy back soon.

> CARL
>
> Soon as she can. You want baked beans for tea? Make you strong.

CHANTAL appears. CARL sits cuddling JASMINE, who pats the dog. CHANTAL stays standing.

> CHANTAL
>
> Mummy'll soon be home, won't she Carl?

CARL nods, struggling to control his emotions.

**CHANTAL (CONT'D)**
It wasn't your fault Carl. She looked the wrong way. It was an accident.

CARL nods, gets up and goes to the kitchenette. He busies himself with making JASMINE's tea, opening a can of beans and toasting sliced white bread. JASMINE plays with the dog.

**CARL**
Just wish she'd trusted me.

**CHANTAL**
We never did anything, Carl. When she hears about me and Pete it'll all be OK.

**CARL**
Dunno about that. Ready for your tea, princess? Daddy's strong girl?

JASMINE jumps up, displaying her arm muscles. They laugh. CHANTAL's phone buzzes. She checks it.

**CHANTAL**
I gotta go. Pete and I'll call soon, right?

CHANTAL ruffles JASMINE's hair and leaves. CARL spoons baked beans onto toast onto a plate and puts it on the table.

JASMINE skips over and sits on her booster seat. CARL grabs two apples. He munches one, slicing the other, and arranges it in a rabbit bowl, as JASMINE starts eating.

CARL
That nice, princess?

JASMINE nods, eats a few mouthfuls and pushes the plate away.

CARL
Mummy be better soon.

JASMINE
Yes all better. Apple now Daddy.


END

..........................................................

Heather De Lyon has worked in teaching, training, social work, community work and project management, and is passionate about increasing social equality. She has written articles for *The Guardian*, *Baby Magazine* and *Spare Rib*, has produced several short films and moved to Norfolk from Hackney, via New Zealand. She has two sons.

# Cynthia Garcia

Layla Gets a Treat

FADE IN:

INT./EXT. LAYLA'S BEDROOM/DRIVEWAY – DAY

LAYLA, a chubby 14 year old with tissues stuffed up her nose, is peeking out her bedroom blinds.

She's watching her mother, LUCY, 30, a smartly dressed woman, unlocking and getting into a red Lexus.

The Chicago suburb is on the wealthier side, filled with tall hedges and protective fences. Lucy and Layla's house has neither.

Layla lets the blinds free once the car pulls out of the driveway and is out of sight.

INT./EXT. KITCHEN/ROAD – DAY

Layla, tissues still stuffed up her nose, goes to open the fridge, but notices a couple of Post-it notes on the door. She looks around. There are more Post-its on the cabinets, the oven, the microwave and around the stove.

A white and brown greyhound, BANJO, is sprawled on the kitchen floor. Even he has a Post-it note on his collar.

She skims some of the notes on the fridge door as the cuckoo clock near the fridge TICKS.

**INSERT: LAYLA'S POV:**

One note says: 'Are you hungry or just bored?'

Another: 'An apple will make you healthier. Ice cream will make you worse.'

**BACK TO SCENE**

Layla sighs.

She opens the fridge and grabs an apple. She takes a bite. It's crisp.

She blankly stares out the window and half-heartedly chews for a couple of seconds. TICK. TICK. TICK.

Outside, an old Toyota Corolla slowly RATTLES on by.

Banjo is awake and scratching at the sliding door wanting to be let out. His Post-it note falls on the floor.

The cuckoo clock goes off.

Layla picks up Banjo's Post-it.

**INSERT: LAYLA'S POV:**

'I like to go outside at 9:30am.'

**BACK TO SCENE**

The clock is striking 10am.

The taste of the apple isn't worth it. She spits whatever bit of apple she had left onto the Post-it note in her hand.

She opens the sliding door for Banjo and throws the apple and the Post-it note outside.

                    **LAYLA**
            Go get it Banjo-lina Jolie!

Banjo happily runs after them.

**INT. LIVING ROOM – DAY**

Layla is sitting cross-legged on the living room floor flipping through television channels. There is a soda can in her hand and next to her is an open bag of chips. MUSIC is coming from a white iPhone that is on the couch.

She stops on a random channel to take a big gulp of soda. Her eyes widen when she sees the channel information.

**INSERT: LAYLA'S POV:**

*'SEXY SLUTS IN OUTER SPACE'*

**BACK TO SCENE**

She takes the tissues out of her nose, puts her soda can down and stares. Her jaw drops as we hear GIGGLES, loud KISSING, and MOANING. She is entranced. Then the doorbell RINGS.

Layla is startled and scrambles to turn off the TV. She shuts off the music for good measure.

## EXT. FRONT DOOR – DAY

The old Toyota Corolla is parked on the street.

A YOUNG MAN, 19, wearing jeans and a cardigan with a leather satchel hanging off of one shoulder, is standing in front of the home's big wooden door.

He is nervously fiddling with his satchel's strap. He's trying to look into the house's front window, but the drapes are closed.

## INT. HALLWAY – DAY

Layla creeps towards the front door. She flinches when there's KNOCKING at the door.

She looks through the peephole.

## INSERT: THROUGH THE PEEPHOLE:

Layla's POV of the young man.

## BACK TO SCENE

She looks away and scrunches up her face as if trying to place him. She can't, but decides to look through the peephole again.

## INSERT: THROUGH THE PEEPHOLE:

He's gone, but she notices the Toyota Corolla parked in front of her house.

## BACK TO SCENE

She quickly glances into the living room towards the kitchen. The sliding door is still open.

She bounds up the stairs.

**EXT. BACKYARD – DAY**

The young man climbs over the wooden fence that surrounds the backyard.

When he drops down, he is greeted happily by Banjo.

The young man smiles and pets Banjo. He notices pieces of the Post-it note on Banjo's mouth and takes them off. He chuckles and gives Banjo another pat on the head.

His smile widens when he notices the sliding door is open.

**INT./EXT. LUCY'S BEDROOM/BACKYARD – DAY**

Layla runs in and locks the door. She is out of breath and sniffling. She grabs some more tissues from her pocket and stuffs them up her nose.

Her mother's room has one window overlooking the driveway; a second window overlooks the backyard.

She freezes when she hears the sliding door pushed further open.

She closes her eyes and listens.

There are careful footsteps.

Drawers are being opened and rummaged through.

Layla opens her eyes and her hands go immediately to her pockets. Whatever she was hoping to find, isn't there.

**INT. LIVING ROOM – DAY**

The young man spots Layla's white iPhone on the couch. He picks it up and inspects it. It's good. He slips it into his satchel.

He also notices the bag of chips, soda and used tissues on the floor. He looks around worriedly.

> **YOUNG MAN**
> (calling)
> Lucy? You home?

**INT. LUCY'S BEDROOM – DAY**

Layla is confused, but she doesn't respond.

**INT. LIVING ROOM – DAY**

The young man waits for a response. When he doesn't get one he's relieved and continues to rummage.

**INT. LUCY'S BEDROOM – DAY**

Layla hears the rummaging resume. She quietly opens her mother's closet. She's looking for anything that can help her. Nothing but clothes. She closes it.

She turns to the nightstand. It has three drawers.

The first is filled with a bag of cough drops, a journal, a calculator and a bookkeeping ledger.

She closes it.
The second is in disarray. A bunch of junk mail, bills, and coupons.

She closes it.

The third has a black box with several small boxes beside it. The black box has a Post-it note on it.

Layla has never been happier to see a Post-it note in her life. She kneels and picks up the black box to read the note.

**INSERT: LAYLA'S POV:**

'REMEMBER: EMERGENCY ONLY!!!'

**BACK TO SCENE**

The stairs CREAK. Someone is coming up the stairs.

Layla starts to breathe hard.

She stares at the door.

The footsteps come closer.

**INT. LANDING – DAY**

The young man turns the door handle. It's locked.

      **YOUNG MAN**
 Hmm.

He crouches to inspect the doorknob.

It has a circular keyhole.

He opens up his satchel and looks through it.

INT. LUCY'S BEDROOM – DAY

Layla hears the movement outside and looks again at the box in her hands.

INT. LANDING – DAY

He pulls out a small stack of papers held together by a paperclip. He takes the paperclip and unbends it. He pokes around the tiny hole until the lock POPS.

INT. LUCY'S BEDROOM – DAY

The door swings open. Layla is nervously pointing a gun at the young man, tissues still stuffed up her nose.

The young man freezes in horror. He puts his hands up.

                **YOUNG MAN**
Don't!

                **LAYLA**
... Why!?

Layla continues pointing the gun at him. They stare at each other, trying to figure out each other's next move.

                **YOUNG MAN**
I know your mom!

                **LAYLA**
Huh?... how?

                **YOUNG MAN**
We sort of go out.

**LAYLA**
What? Then why are you robbing us!?

**YOUNG MAN**
Funny story, but can you stop pointing that thing at me? Please?

The young man motions her to put the gun down. Layla nods and lowers the gun slowly.

**YOUNG MAN**
You see, this was just a dare.

As she's about to put it down, a sneeze starts to build. She sneezes. The tissues fly out of her nose and she accidentally pulls the trigger.

The shot hits him in the hip and he crumbles to the floor.

Downstairs, Banjo is wildly BARKING. Layla carefully puts the gun on the floor and hurries to the young man.

**LAYLA**
I am SO sorry!

He is still alive, but injured. He can only groan.

Banjo runs up the stairs to her. She ignores him. Her focus is on the young man. Layla looks at the blood around him in terror. Banjo licks the blood, and Layla quickly shoves him away.

She notices her phone peeking out of the satchel. She grabs the phone and dials 911.

She puts the phone up to her ear, and clears her throat. Layla wants to say something to him, but is unsure of what to say.

**LAYLA**
                (to the young man)
          Uh ... let's not tell my mom, OK?

The young man groans and Banjo starts to lick the blood again.

                                        **FADE OUT**


                            **END**




................................................

Cynthia Garcia was born and raised in Los Angeles, California. She's a Mexican-American screenwriter, sketch writer and sometimes actress.

# Tim Lawrence

## Telling Tales
*An edited extract from a short play*

In the aftermath of a medieval feast a tavern **WENCH** tries to choose with whom to spend the night, **1ST KNIGHT** or **2ND KNIGHT**.

*2nd Knight drops a heavy coin purse on the table.*
*Wench smiles at 2nd Knight and picks up the purse.*
*She smiles at the 1st Knight and holds out her empty hand.*
*1st Knight drops his coin purse into her palm.*
*Wench compares the weight of both purses.*

**Wench**
Hmm. Two men of equal weight, how am I to choose?

**2nd Knight**
Madam, I have seen the candle of my brother's passion. The flame burns quickly and the wick is soon left drooping.

**1st Knight**
Most crude sir. Where is it you have seen my passion falter so?

**2nd Knight**
On the field sir.

**1st Knight**
On the field? Do you mean to say I am a coward?

**2nd Knight**

No sir. No coward is my brother, therefore no brother a coward. Your valor is true and just as any king. However the strength of your sword …

**Wench**

Gentlemen, you joust like children. Step off your wooden horses.

**1st Knight**

Saint George is in my sword and I come to return him to the heart of every heathen. This land was once his so I shall bring him into every home we pass and they shall know Saint George again. My shield carries the antlers of Saint Eustance, should I find myself alone on the field, as long as I have Saint Eustance at my side my faith shall not be shaken.

**Wench**

My good knight, you use your tongue very well. Sir, can you move your tongue with as much skill?

**2nd Knight**

Madam, I fear I cannot show my weapons such eloquent poetry. I wear a sword on the field but I seldom draw it, and I have no shield to brag of. My weapon is a pike and its size is so much greater than the sword it requires both hands for expert use.

**Wench**

Ha, a sharp tongue to match a subtle one. This is a choice indeed. Very well, you shall prove the worth of your tongues and then I shall judge with whom to spend the night. Do you both consent to my contest?

**1st Knight**

A contest of tongues? I fear the wine addles my mind. Madam, state more plainly the terms of your contest.

**Wench**
A story contest, sirs. Each will tell a story and I shall judge whose is best. That man shall win the prize. I ask though no stories of saints and martyrs. Such pure and godly men hold no place in such a contest as ours.

**1st Knight**
Ah, then I have a tale for us! When I was a child my nurse asked me did I know of the lord and of the old gentleman.

*2nd Knight groans, he's heard this tale before.*

**1st Knight**
I answered the lord was God, my creator, my keeper, but I knew not of the old gentleman. Then I must tell you of him. In the village of my birth, once lived a blacksmith well renowned for his skills. This blacksmith liked to play dice. Each night after his work was done he'd sit and roll dice in the village inn, often winning. One night after he'd taken three men's money from them he stood and toasted the inn with a drunken boast, 'I am a blacksmith and I have mastered fire! The old gentleman himself is not such a master!' That night as the blacksmith walked towards his home he spied a lone figure at the side of the path. An old man, dressed all in black, hunched over a long black coffin, upon which he rolled a single die.

*The 2nd Knight sneaks behind the Wench.*

**1st Knight**
He smiled at the blacksmith and held out the die.

**2nd Knight**
*(To Wench)* Play me. If you win I'll give you all the wealth I possess, if you lose you'll help me carry this coffin.

**1st Knight**
> The blacksmith, still bold from his winning at the inn and greedy for more, accepted the old man's challenge. He took the die and rolled it thrice. Six, three, five. Not a bad score. The old man took back the die and rolled it once, six. Out in the darkness an owl gave a shriek. The old man rolled again, six. A toad began to croak. The old man cast the die a third time, it span on its edge refusing to fall. As it span, bats beat the air with their wings till the blacksmith thought dragons were bearing down upon him. Then suddenly the noise stopped; the die had fallen. Six. The old man smiled, took back his die and stood; 'now you must help me carry the coffin.' The blacksmith had no choice.

> *1st Knight lifts a chair onto his shoulder.*

**1st Knight**
> He lifted the coffin onto his shoulder and began walking towards the graveyard. As he walked the blacksmith heard the clop, clop, clop of hooves on the cobbles. He stopped, so did the hooves. He looked over his shoulder; the old man smiling was all he could see. The blacksmith looked ahead and walked on.

> *2nd Knight bangs his cup on the table. Clop, clop, clop.*

**1st Knight**
> A shiver ran down the blacksmith's spine. As they walked through the headstones the bones of the dead rattled in their graves.

> *1st Knight puts down the chair.*

They laid the coffin down and the old man handed the blacksmith a spade, 'you must dig the grave.' The blacksmith couldn't speak to answer. He shook his head. The old man's smile grew, 'I'll tell you a riddle, answer me right and you can go your way. What lies in the dark and cannot scratch its nose, nor reach down to touch its toes?' The blacksmith stared at the old man without an answer. 'Dig.' The blacksmith put his foot to the spade and dug the grave.

*1st Knight looks to 2nd Knight.*

**1st Knight**
When he finished he asked the old man, 'what is the answer?'

*2nd Knight points at the chair.*

**1st Knight**
The old man said nothing but pointed to the coffin. The blacksmith knelt beside the coffin; his fingers trembled as he placed his hands upon it.

*1st Knight kneels beside the chair. 2nd Knight moves behind him.*

**1st Knight**
Biting his lip, he threw back the lid. The coffin was empty. (*2nd Knight grabs 1st Knights by the neck*). Suddenly the old man seized the blacksmith by the scruff of his neck and lifted him high off the ground. The old man's eyes blazed with fire, his smile sharp with fangs as he flung the blacksmith into the coffin and slammed down the lid.

*1st Knight drops to his knees and slams his fists into the chair.*

The blacksmith lay pinned in darkness as the old gentleman rapped on the coffin, 'can you scratch your nose blacksmith? Can you reach down to touch your toes?' The old man dragged the coffin to the grave and pushed it in. He buried the blacksmith. As he was buried, the blacksmith began to laugh; with each shovel of earth his laughter grew. Even when the grave was full and the old man had disappeared, faint laughter could still be heard. They say even now, if you walk through that graveyard at midnight you can still hear the blacksmith laughing at his foolishness.

**Wench**
A fine story, my good knight.

**2nd Knight**
Told almost as well as the last time, thought not quite as well as the time before that.

*He stares into his cup.*

I have a new tale. I was told this story by a young girl in the last village our company stopped. A great Turk king, long ago, had a daughter beautiful as the desert skies at night, but no sons to carry on his reign. He sent forth a proclamation to all parts of his realm saying he would give his daughter's hand to any man, high or low, who could prove himself worthy. A peasant boy from a desert village heard this proclamation. He went to his grandmother, the eldest woman in the village, and asked her, 'Grandmother, what could I do to prove my worth to a king?' The old woman's ancient lips cracked open in a toothless smile. 'Out in the desert, when you have walked into the setting sun for a full month, you will find a monstrous vine that fills half the desert. From this vine hangs a single crop of grapes. It is said the smallest taste of this fruit could melt the heart of the fiercest tyrant.'

*He stands.*

The boy leapt to his feet, 'I shall do it! I shall find this fruit and win myself a princess!' The old woman raised a wrinkled hand, 'wait child! Thousands of young men have sought this fruit through the generations, none has ever returned. The fruit is a treasure and a curse, you must never eat more than a single grape at a time.' That night the boy walked out into the desert, chasing the setting sun. The boy walked across the hot sands for a full month, till one morning he climbed a dune and looked down on a desert filled by a monstrous vine. He climbed down into the vine. The thorns scratched at his face and tore his clothing but he pushed through. After two days of struggling through the vine the boy reached a clearing. In the centre, hanging from a single vine, was a single crop of grapes. The boy reached up and picked the grapes. He squeezed their juice into a flask and mashed the grapes into a paste. He pushed back through the vine. After another month of walking through the desert he reached the king's palace. He stood before the king, a lone peasant boy, dusty and tired from his journey, trembling as he offered the ruler of men a single drink from a leather flask. The king laughed as a few drops were poured into his glass.

*He pours wine into the Wench's cup.*

But as he raised the glass to his lips and smelt the fragrance, tasted the sweet juice, silence filled the court. The king put down his glass and summoned his daughter. The boy was taken, washed with fine oils, dressed in beautiful robes and brought back before the king. The king took the boy's hand and placed in it the hand of his daughter (he puts the 1st Knight's hand into the Wench's). 'Daughter, most precious jewel of my life, I give you to this man who has proven himself worthy. Go with my blessing and make him a prince.' The boy looked into the princess's eyes and kissed her for the first time. They walked from the palace hand in hand, and were carried off on a golden litter. That night as they shared a bed for the first time, the boy fed his princess a few drops of the juice. The princess begged for another drink. The boy smiled, 'tomorrow night you may have more.' They slept in each other's arms. The next night again the boy fed her a few drops of the juice, again she begged for another drink. Again the boy smiled, 'tomorrow you may have more.' That night the princess woke and slipped from the bed. She took the flask, removed the cork and lifted it to her lips. She drank, and drank, and found herself unable to stop such was the ecstasy of the juice. She drank every last drop. As she lowered the flask she felt a tingling at her fingertips. It spread up her arms, across her chest, through her belly and down her legs. Her body began to stretch and twist. Her arms spread across the room, her legs crawled away from her over the floor. The next morning the boy awoke to find a vine stretched over the bed. Hanging from the vine was a single crop of grapes.

..................................................

Tim Lawrence started making things up at an early age. At some point he learned how to use a pen, so now he writes them down. Tim loves myths, legends, and storytelling. He has a blog of short stories, which he'll keep writing until someone pays him to stop.
www.tellthemtales.blogspot.co.uk

# Gytha Lodge

Dying for Darwin

Thirteen-year-old Danny's dad was a Darwin Award winner for dying in the most humiliating of circumstances: naked at an AC/DC gig in front of millions. Films of his death became a YouTube sensation, but Danny is left trying to deal with his grief when he can't escape the footage or the laughter.

*Lights up to show the front of a huge red train, which looks as though it has crashed through the back of the stage. It will loom over every scene.*

*A crowd cheers in the distance, and (very quietly) AC/DC's* Touch Too Much *plays. There is a surge of noise, then, as if from a distance, DANNY's overlaid voice yells in anguish.*

**DANNY:** Dad!

*Lights up on the foreground. There are two cheap padded chairs that schools go in for in waiting areas. They look comfy but aren't. Between them is a low, plastic-topped coffee table with a square box of tissues on it.*

*To SR, a free-standing door complete with frame.*

*ROB WOODS, a young history teacher, is sitting with a stack of essays and a cup of coffee. DANNY opens the door, sees ROB, and starts to retreat. He is just 13, has a split lip and a bruise on his jaw, and is tense but closed-off.*

**ROB:** All right, Danny?

DANNY: Yeah. Yeah, fine.

*He retreats, closing the door behind him, and leaves the lit area.*

*MARTINA arrives moments later, and walks in, a little flustered. She stops on seeing ROB.*

ROB: Oh, sorry. Are you in here this afternoon?

MARTINA: Yes. Sorry, it's every Tuesday.

ROB: I'll move. I'm nearly done anyway, but the staff room is full of sweaty PE teachers.

MARTINA: (getting her coat off) I used to hate my PE teacher.

ROB: (as he packs away) Are you seeing Danny? You should feel honoured. He's sort of famous around here. Did you know his dad managed to hang himself naked at an –

MARTINA: Yes, thank you.

ROB: Oh. Oh, I suppose that's why you're – well it must be ... hard.

*He realises his double entendre, and tries very hard to keep a serious expression, and then snorts with laughter.*

Sorry. I know it's heartless. But honestly ... What a prick!

*MARTINA tries to glare at him, but she is finding it hard not to laugh too.*

*Pause.*

MARTINA: You have kids?

**ROB:** Oh, two, yes.

**MARTINA:** How old?

**ROB:** Ten and four.

**MARTINA:** What do you think could help them? If it'd been you who'd died in front of millions of people, with an erection?

**ROB:** I don't think I'm likely to ... never had that sort of sense of humour, if that's what you could call it.

**MARTINA:** No, I suppose not.

*He exits.*

*After MARTINA has checked her watch, DANNY returns, and knocks this time.*

**MARTINA:** Come in.

*DANNY enters, looking mulish.*

**MARTINA:** Did you come before I got here? So sorry I was late. I managed to lock myself out of the car.

*DANNY sits without replying. He doesn't look at her.*

*MARTINA's phone suddenly goes off, playing a tinny version of* Touch Too Much. *She scrambles in her bag.*

**MARTINA:** Gosh, sorry. Thought I'd turned it ...

*She switches it off.*

**MARTINA:** So how's your week been?

*DANNY shrugs.*

MARTINA: Anything you'd like to talk about?

DANNY: I don't need to tell you when they've already told you.

MARTINA: Being told you've been vandalising and fighting isn't the same as you telling me what happened.

DANNY: Why not?

MARTINA: I'd like to know your take on it, and why you did what you did. I'm sure there were reasons. Would you like to tell me?

DANNY: I just fucking hate fairy lights, all right?

MARTINA: And what about the fight?

DANNY: Look, will you just leave it? I'm fed up of talking about it.

MARTINA: All right.

*Pause.*

MARTINA: How's your work going? I'm still hearing really good things about your art.

DANNY: Yeah, it's OK. Maths is crap, though, and Clements is a twat.

MARTINA: You're not the first person who's said so. How do you get on with Mr Grey?

DANNY: He's a loser. He's all trying to be cool all the time. He keeps saying 'like' cos he thinks that's how we talk, 'like.' Man's a joke.

MARTINA: But he's supportive? Doesn't jump down your throat or anything?

DANNY: No, he's all right.

*Pause. She sits, waiting patiently, allowing the silence to stretch on.*

DANNY: Look, you're always – you're always trying to get me to talk about my dad, but I know you know what happened, all right? They would've thought you should know.

MARTINA: What do you think I should know about it?

DANNY: I don't know ... Why don't you just go and watch it on YouTube? Save me the bother.

MARTINA: I'd like to hear what you have to say, instead.

DANNY: Bet you've fucking watched it anyway.

*He tries to read her and fails, gives up.*

DANNY: I'm not in the mood, OK?

MARTINA: OK.

DANNY: You're supposed to ask me why I destroyed all that shit and if I'm sorry.

MARTINA: Really?

DANNY: Yeah.

MARTINA: Would you like me to?

DANNY: Stop asking me what I'd like. I'd like to be out playing football and not stuck in here, all right?

**MARTINA:** All right. You're free to go if you want.

*Pause.*

**DANNY:** What, really?

**MARTINA:** Of course. It's not detention. I'm here to listen when you want to talk to me.

**DANNY:** About the fight?

**MARTINA:** About anything.

**DANNY:** I just ... I lost my temper.

*RYAN and EWAN tumble on, and DANNY stands and turns away from them, keeping his head down.*

**RYAN:** Hey, Danny! You want to see a bit of something to turn you on? Hey, Danny! Oy.

*He grabs him around the shoulders, as if friendly, but with a roughness that clearly almost hurts. DANNY tries to pretend it's fine.*

**RYAN:** Look what I've got on my phone. This your kind of thing?

*DANNY doesn't look at the phone he holds out, and doesn't answer.*

**RYAN:** Don't you like porn, Danny? What are you, a fag or something?

**EWAN:** Look, he's blushing.

**RYAN:** Are you a fag?

**DANNY:** No.

**RYAN:** Come on then, prove it.

DANNY: No.

RYAN: You'll love it, Danny. It's your dad's cock.

*Quite suddenly, DANNY loses it. He delivers a swift, short punch to RYAN's face and then follows it up by punching him in the stomach and pushing him over. He tries to kick him, but EWAN grabs him and then tries to get him in a headlock.*

*DANNY kicks him in the shin, and has fought free when MRS LETHERBY walks on.*

MRS LETHERBY: You hold it there. I will not have fighting in my school. Go to my office, Danny. Go to my office. You two can talk to Mr Singh about what happened.

*DANNY goes and sits down again, tense and clearly upset.*

MARTINA: You were very angry with him, weren't you?

DANNY: Course I was. What's his fucking problem? He's dead and he thinks it's OK to take the piss. I fucking hate him.

MARTINA: Ryan?

DANNY: Dad. I fucking hate him. Why did he have to do that? It's so stupid. It's so stupid.

*He is crying, snottily. MARTINA reaches for the box of tissues on the table and hands him one. DANNY grabs at it.*

MARTINA: It's OK to be angry.

DANNY: No it isn't. Mum says it's the last thing she needs now, when everything's so crap. She was so pissed off when I wrecked the Christmas tree at Auntie Sarah's.

MARTINA: Didn't you tell her why you'd done it?

DANNY: No.

MARTINA: You can always tell me, if you want to.

DANNY: I was just – I woke up in the night and I wanted a drink, and I guess I was – you know, half asleep still. And someone had left the Christmas tree on. And cos I wasn't properly awake, the way the lights were all wrapped round it, it looked like Dad. Before he ran out onto the stage.

MARTINA: What happened?

DANNY: Mum came downstairs and turned the light on, and I realised it was just a fucking tree.

MARTINA: So you knocked it over?

DANNY: Yeah. No. I tore it to pieces.

MARTINA: And your mum was angry?

DANNY: Course she was. She thought Auntie Sarah'd throw us out. But I couldn't really hear her, you know like when you're really focused on one thing and everything else just vanishes?

MARTINA: Yes.

DANNY: So she hit me round the head and I woke up. I almost hit her back. And then she started bawling because she doesn't believe in hitting. But I – I know I should have said sorry or something, but she started asking why I didn't stop him. It's all she ever asks me about it, why I didn't stop him.

MARTINA: Sometimes people react strangely when they're grieving, Danny. And really, I'm sure she doesn't blame you. She's just looking for someone to be angry with.

*DANNY remains silent.*

MARTINA: Have you and your mum spoken about how you feel?

DANNY: She won't talk about him.

MARTINA: Have you talked to her about how that makes you feel?

DANNY: No! It's not – you can't just say 'I'm feeling really sad about that.'

MARTINA: Why not?

DANNY: Because it's not – nobody says that sort of shit. It's bollocks.

MARTINA: How do you talk about things with your mum, then?

DANNY: I just – I just ... I don't.

MARTINA: Not about anything?

DANNY: No.

MARTINA: Do you tell her how your day's been?

DANNY: Course I do. I just ... I tell her it was fine. Or I want to go to Matt's.

MARTINA: I see.

| | |
|---|---|
| **DANNY:** | I didn't really think it was Dad. Not really. Like, I looked at them lights ... I wanted it to be Dad, but I didn't ... |

*Pause.*

| | |
|---|---|
| **MARTINA:** | Do you talk to Matt? |
| **DANNY:** | What about? |
| **MARTINA:** | About the things that make you unhappy. |
| **DANNY:** | He's a mate. You don't – sometimes, yeah. But not, like ... I don't tell him all the time. He knows I'm upset about it, but he doesn't ask much. Just once, really. |

*He stands, and goes to SL. MATT walks on with a pair of chairs. He turns them to face SL and they both slouch in them. A projector in the wings casts the moving lights of a screen on them, and sound comes on at the same time, making it clear they're watching* Taken.

| | |
|---|---|
| **MATT:** | Do you ever miss your dad? |
| **DANNY:** | Nah ... Yeah. Sometimes. You? |
| **MATT:** | Not really. I mean, he was a prick, you know? And he used to tell Mum and Stace what to do all the time so ... you know, good riddance. |
| **DANNY:** | Yeah. |
| **MATT:** | He tried to phone me last week, but I told him to fuck off. |
| **DANNY:** | Right. |
| **MATT:** | He had some Cup Final tickets, he said, but he said that last year about those fake ones. |

DANNY:          Oh yeah. And he got arrested.

MATT:           Yeah, and I had to get a cab home with my lunch money and Mum went spare. Like I would – I would sort of like to see him, though. Cos he used to listen when I complained about Mum being obsessed with tidying everything and he understood. And he was all right to kick a ball around with, you know?

DANNY:          Yeah.

MATT:           Can you imagine him ever doing this shit, though? Rescuing Stace from kidnappers? He'd run a fucking mile, you know?

DANNY:          Yeah. My dad ... He would have done it, maybe. And he probably would've been funnier than Liam Neeson, but you know ... not scary. And actually, he probably would've tripped over and shot himself or something.

MATT:           (laughing) Yeah. He probably would've.

*There is a pause while DANNY wipes at his eyes, then stands up, and goes back to sit with MARTINA.*

..........................................

Gytha Lodge is a full-time novelist and scriptwriter, with two national theatre writing awards and several shortlistings under her belt, as well as a sell-out run at Leicester Square Theatre's best of fringe season. She is currently writing a TV drama and a YA fantasy series. She is represented by Curtis Brown.

# Emma Maclusky

The Waiter

*Restaurant.*

*Michael, 32, seated alone at a table. Next to him are a young couple trying to enjoy their meal. Michael is writing on a napkin. A large glass of wine and an empty bottle sit on the table. He holds up the napkin he has been writing on, the picture resembles a tree.*

**Michael**

Here you, this is it. I've traced it back as far as I can. I didn't twig at first either, but it makes sense doesn't it? I'll hang onto this if that's OK?

*Michael puts the napkin on the table and straightens his shirt.*

It's 20.08. No, scratch that. 20.09. How long I been here? One hour and nine minutes. I'll give it another ten minutes. Fifteen. What did you choose? Avoid the pasta – they put something weird like anchovies in it. Oh you got the pasta.

*Michael creates a swan out of the napkin.*

I want to know, what would it be like if you could steal someone else's time? Just an hour or two from their life. Like that kid and his mum over there. He has spaghetti all over his face and hands and is seconds away from wiping them on his mother's white dress. But she doesn't care. She's just smiling at him. Imagine, just for an hour, knowing what it is like to be him. No matter how messy you get, she doesn't care. It's crazy how they are made from the same stuff, too. Like DNA, flesh and blood that's crazy. Flesh is a horrid word. I can't feel my face. Look at them. Completely in tune. They're the same.

*Michael tries to stand the swan up but it falls over. He sighs.*

Did you know that when pianos are placed in a room together ... when you play them they start to tune to each other, to the same note? It doesn't matter how far apart you take them and what they have been through. They don't sound right when they're on their own; they're flat or sharp. Put them in one place together and they create something special. Something real. Because they're all connected, made from the same stuff.

*Pause.*

I thought she'd come this time. I ironed my shirt. The waiters want me to move to the bar. Why? There is only room for one at the bar. I'm waiting. You don't mind me being here, do you? I'll wait another ten minutes. Fifteen. I'll wait fifteen. So, have you been here before?

*Michael folds the napkin neatly into a hat. He picks up the wine bottle and looks at it.*

Does this shirt look ironed to you? What am I asking you for? You're a bottle. Does it look ironed to you?

*Michael puts the hat on.*

Happy Birthday, Michael.

*Michael takes the hat off and makes a paper airplane.*

She'll come. She has to. It's not about money, I would have paid. I saved especially. I guess I'll put it back in the swear jar. I don't usually swear, haven't said fuck or shit at all today. Well, it has been working, I've nearly gone the whole day. I don't want to use the money for anything else, I saved it for her. She said she'd be here. She probably got held up at work or stuck in traffic. It's kind of like when a parent is late to pick you up from school. You can't help but feel a little cheated of your time. She said she'd fucking be here.

*Michael puts a coin on the table.*

Another for the jar. Shit. It doesn't really suit my personality, does it? I wanted to show people I could swear. It is possible for someone like me to talk like that. I don't have to be a gentleman all the time, and it's quite liberating, actually, calms me down. I would never do anything outrageous, but throwing in the occasional shit wank fuck bugger titty bum does feel good. She didn't like it, either. She said it sounded dirty, horrible. Thick. So I've been trying to stop. If she was here, she could see for herself. I hardly ever swear. Last time we saw each other, I hadn't ironed my shirt. And I swore. And I didn't pay for anything. That's changed. People can change, you know? If you give them time to. You need the time, just a moment. A moment to show that you've got something worth noticing. Oh they're going. The mother and her kid. He's holding her hand.

*Michael flies the paper airplane which flops pathetically. He looks at the empty place opposite him.*

First time I saw her, she didn't look at all how I imagined. She looked tired and strained. A bit like a tea towel that's been wound up, ready to whip someone. When she smiled, it was a bit unnatural, like she had gotten good at practising happiness. I thought she'd look like me. I was so fucking nervous. I knew a bit about her before, of course. Her emails said about her job, where she lives. That's when I put the tree together.

*Michael looks at the napkin.*

Do you mind me talking like this? I suppose I have moved to the bar. I hope I haven't ruined your meal. Do you want more wine? I don't usually drink wine. I had pictured it in my head, played out the conversations we would have over and over. But one thing I didn't think of was the silence. And the steely look she gave me. I thought there would be more hugs and choked conversations about the years lost. It was more like a business meeting. But it'll get better. I'm better this time. Well, I make the effort.

*Michael downs his drink. He untucks his shirt.*

I'm not angry at her. I'm over it; ready to start again. I should be mad. I should be fucking livid. Dumping a baby in a trolley at Asda and leaving him in the car park in the rain is pretty fucking bad. It wasn't even a nice supermarket. I mean, if you're going to dump someone at a supermarket at least choose a nice one like Waitrose. Fucking Asda. But hey, she had issues, she was under pressures, I can't judge. But if I've managed to turn up, dressed like a poof and wait for an hour then the least she could do, out of guilt, is to turn up. I'm not angry. Not at her.

*A man in a tailcoat suit starts playing a grand piano at the back of the restaurant, a classical and beautiful tune.*

Fucking great. It's fucking beautiful, isn't it?

*Michael hums along, completely the wrong song and out of tune.*

I thought I'd be able to call her Mum by now. Not even close.

Well, maybe next year. She'll come next year. I should probably leave. Fuck it. Enjoy the rest of your meal. The pasta really is shit.

*Michael gets up to leave. He looks at the empty place opposite him. He stops and sits down. He tucks in his shirt.*

Ten more minutes. Fifteen.

..........................................

Emma Maclusky studied BA Scriptwriting and Performance at the University of East Anglia. During her degree, she wrote three short plays, which were staged, two full-length plays, and two radio plays that were broadcast around campus. She recently worked with a local theatre company, Stuff of Dreams, through which her first full-length play was staged, *Love Left Hanging*, with 10 tour dates across Norfolk, Suffolk, Leicester and finishing at the Brighton Fringe Festival in May.

# Faith Ng

Skin

*The art studio is immaculately clean. There are paintbrushes, tubes of paint, and pieces of cloth lying on the floor but, even then, the mess looks neat. Hanging on the walls are canvases of different sizes. They show incomplete attempts to paint different faces. Two men, LIM (30) and FRANCIS (25), stand in front of these paintings.*

**LIM:** I grew up watching my mother dress up to go to work every morning. She would be seated at the dressing table, her hair wrapped in a white towel, staring at herself in the mirror as she applied make-up to her face. My favourite part of this routine was when she quietly held out her tube of bright red lipstick and looked at me. Without exchanging a single word, I would take the lipstick from her and apply it carefully over her lips. When I was done, I would pass the lipstick back to her, and she would look in the mirror and smile with such surprise and delight at the sight of her freshly made-up face. And then she would look at me and smile, as though I had just done a spectacular magic trick, as though I had given her a new face and new skin. But I got greedy, over the years. I wanted the magic to extend to me. One morning, after she had gotten ready, I sat at her dressing table and applied her lipstick to my lips. As I was doing this, I saw her, through the mirror, staring at me with horror written all over her lovely face. We never talked about it. And I never did it again.

**FRANCIS:** You've never told me this before.

**LIM:** I forgot about it myself ... I only just recalled it.

**FRANCIS:** How's she doing?

**LIM:** The chemo seems to be working.

**FRANCIS:** That's good.

**LIM:** Yeah.

*LIM looks at the paintings on the wall.*

**LIM:** Do you want any of them?

**FRANCIS:** You've not finished any of them.

**LIM:** I'm not going to paint anymore.

**FRANCIS:** You're not?

**LIM:** No. I've been afraid to tell you this, but it's no good hiding it anymore – I can't paint. I think I've lost it – the gift, or whatever it was.

**FRANCIS:** Maybe it's because you stopped letting me be with you while you paint. You always said I was your muse.

**LIM:** Anyway, I can't paint anymore. My mother needs

| | |
|---|---|
| | me. I'm going to sell this space and move back home to look after her. |
| FRANCIS: | You're giving up? |
| LIM: | No … I'm growing up, that's all. It's time to live in the real world. You should too. |
| FRANCIS: | I am living in the real world. |
| LIM: | No you're not. People stare at you all the time. |
| FRANCIS: | Let them stare. |
| LIM: | People laugh at you. |
| FRANCIS: | I don't care. |
| LIM: | I do. |
| FRANCIS: | Well, we're not together anymore so fuck you. Go run back to Mummy and hide between her legs. |
| LIM: | What's wrong with you? |
| FRANCIS: | Is there really no room for me at all in your new world? |
| LIM: | We agreed that we would be mature about this. |
| FRANCIS: | I know. I'm sorry. I just – I can't carry out a normal conversation with you as if nothing is wrong, as if you hadn't just told me that you're leaving me. |
| LIM: | Francis, this is hard for me too. |

FRANCIS: Is it?

LIM: Yes. I'm tired. Of being a secret. I'm tired of being ashamed.

FRANCIS: You don't have to be.

LIM: I'm tired of knowing that there's something wrong with me.

FRANCIS: There's nothing wrong with you.

LIM: I'm tired of being different. I'm tired of having to worry about you, how people look at you, how you reflect upon me, how brave and flamboyant you are, how beautiful you are with your long blond hair and how confident you are in your skin, this stunning skin, this very same skin that I share, that I wish I could tear into shreds so I could rise from it anew and be whole again.

FRANCIS: Lim … *(Holds his hand and gives it a squeeze.)* You are whole.

LIM: *(pushes FRANCIS's hand away)* No. It's wrong. We're wrong. This is wrong.

FRANCIS: You let us be wrong for three whole years?

LIM: I was a coward for three whole years.

FRANCIS: You were brave for three whole years.

*Pause.*

LIM: Perhaps. I'm sorry. You have to let me go. I'm not as strong as you are.

FRANCIS: Don't say that.

LIM: *(smiles)* I remember all the things I painted for you. You inspired me. We were shadows in forgotten corridors, we stole kisses from each other as we walked down crowded streets. Our neighbours cursed us, but we didn't care. Some days we stayed in bed all day, our arms and legs entangled together. We had fun, didn't we?

FRANCIS: We can still make things work.

LIM: Look *(he motions to the canvases on the wall)* at how bare they are. I feel as if I have a paintbrush in my hand, but all the colours have run dry.

*FRANCIS looks at LIM.*

FRANCIS: Why can't you fight harder? For me?

*LIM hears him but does not respond. In anger, FRANCIS marches over to the canvases on the wall. He takes one off the wall and throws it onto the floor.*

LIM: What the hell are you doing?

FRANCIS: I'm sick to death of your self-pity! I'm sick of it!

*FRANCIS moves over to the second canvas, and flings it onto the floor. His fingers curl into hard fists and just as he is about to punch the third canvas, LIM rushes to him and stops him. A struggle ensues for a few seconds. Finally, LIM lets go of FRANCIS. FRANCIS grabs a large tube of red paint from the floor and pushes it into LIM's hand.*

**FRANCIS:** Use it.

**LIM:** Will you stop this!

**FRANCIS:** Use it!

**LIM:** I can't! I can't! I can't paint! I can't do anything anymore!

**FRANCIS:** Use it, Lim! Paint!

*Provoked, LIM glares at FRANCIS. They lock eyes as LIM deliberately squeezes the paint all over his hands, letting it drip down his shirt, pants and shoes.*

**LIM:** Are you happy now? Are you, huh, are you?

**FRANCIS:** *(clapping his hands slowly, sarcastically)* Extremely. You are a masterpiece.

*LIM looks at his stained clothes, and then at the twisted tube of paint in his hands. He throws the tube away in disgust. He backs against the wall and then slides down until he is sitting down and leaning against it.*

**LIM:** Fuck.

*FRANCIS looks at LIM. He takes a piece of cloth and gently and slowly cleans the paint and lipstick off LIM's face. LIM lets him. The paint does not come off; instead it smears LIM's skin even more. FRANCIS persists nevertheless, scrubbing LIM's skin even harder. This takes quite a while.*

**FRANCIS:** When I was growing up, I always felt so embarrassed by my mum. She talked loudly, she was very opinionated, and she had no trouble standing up for herself. I remember once, in Hong Kong, we sat in a small café with a row of computers at the side. We were there for a few hours drinking tea and staring out the window. When the bill came, they had charged us an exorbitant amount of money for using the Internet, even though we hadn't. My mum requested that they remove it from the bill, but they refused. They said, 'Don't you know that this is an Internet café? And that the moment you step foot into this place, you have to pay for the Internet?' The amount of Cantonese vulgarities spewing from her mouth was insane. I felt humiliated by her and the way she handled the matter, even though she was right. I wanted to believe that things, no matter how bad they are, could be handled with grace and tact. And then she passed away. And there was no one left to stand up for me. And I learnt how rude, disgusting and uncaring people can be. How they didn't give a shit about being reasonable, or graceful, or tactful, so all my efforts were wasted on them. I had to learn to do what my mother did – fight hard and fight boldly. It was difficult at first, because I had taught myself the art of blending in and disappearing. But then the more I opened my mouth to speak, the more I got used to the sound of my voice, and it just got louder and louder. Do you know what I'm saying?

*LIM hears him but says nothing.*

**FRANCIS:** Don't run away anymore.

*LIM begins to cry.*

**FRANCIS:** Why are you crying?

**LIM:** I'm sorry.

**FRANCIS:** It's OK.

**LIM:** *(laughs)* Look at me.

**FRANCIS:** What's wrong?

**LIM:** I've stuck a mask onto my face and it can't come off anymore. It's become part of my skin. A new layer of skin drenched in the sweat of my self-pity and self-crucification.

*FRANCIS looks at LIM piteously. He passionately envelops LIM into a tight and warm embrace. LIM fights against it weakly, and then gives in to it.*

**FRANCIS:** *(whispers)* Don't cry … In a less harsh, less judgmental, less conservative, less moralistic place than this, I will give you a name, a character, a life beyond your wildest dreams, and you will stroll languidly around in the blossoming garden of my mind. I will shower you with sweetly decaying affections, as if you were a perfectly manicured porcelain vase. And when you become too good to be true, I will smash you with a hammer and let your beauty, raw and unencumbered, scatter freely over the face of this brown earth.

..................................................

Faith Ng is a Singaporean playwright. Her recent works include *For Better or For Worse* (2013) and *wo(men)* (2010), which was nominated for Best Original Script in *The Straits Times* Life! Theatre Awards (2011). She has also written for the Short & Sweet Festival, National University of Singapore (NUS) Arts Festival and Singapore Arts Festival. She is an Associate Artist with Checkpoint Theatre.

# Luke Wronski

Vitamin G
*An extract from a full-length screenplay*

**INT. JEFF'S LIVING ROOM – LATER**

Jeff emerges from his bedroom into his living room, fully dressed for work. He is wearing black dress pants, a dark green button-up shirt and a brown tie. Nothing matches, but it all looks presentable. He carries with him his gray coat and a briefcase.

Jeff crosses his living room to his adjoining kitchen, which is separated by a counter-top with bar stools on one side.

Jeff leaves his briefcase on the counter and his jacket slung over a bar stool that overlooks the kitchen. He walks into the kitchen and puts on a pot of coffee.

Jeff stands impatiently waiting for his coffee to finish brewing. As he stands gazing dejectedly at his apartment, something suddenly catches his eye.

                        **JEFF**
                  What the hell?

Jeff sees a stranger, lying asleep on his sofa. Cautiously, he walks over and stands in front of the sofa.

The stranger lying there is GOD, 25-looking, shoulder-length hair and a few days' growth on his face. He's dressed in ripped jeans, a faded T-shirt and has his green jacket draped over himself as a makeshift blanket.

Jeff stands awkwardly for a few seconds more, unsure of his next move. Eventually, he picks up a magazine on a nearby coffee table, rolls it up and starts poking the stranger to wake him.

After a few pokes, the stranger rolls back and forth a little bit.

**GOD**
(Groggily)
Fuck off.

Jeff continues to prod.

**GOD (CONT'D)**
Fuck off, man.

Jeff continues to prod, a little harder. God snaps awake and turns to face his prodder, irritated.

**GOD (CONT'D)**
Look, I don't know what the fuck your problem is –

Looks up at Jeff standing over him. His anger fades.

**GOD (CONT'D)**
Oh, it's you.

Tries to wake himself up, gain a bit more awareness of the situation.

**GOD (CONT'D)**
No it's fine. I'm up. I'm up.

God sits up. He rubs his face and looks around at the apartment.

**GOD (CONT'D)**
What time is it?

**JEFF**
Who are you?

**GOD**
What? Didn't I tell you that last night?

**JEFF**
No.

**GOD**
Oh, right. Yeah, I guess I was pretty drunk last night.

**JEFF**
Now who the fuck are you?

**GOD**
Whoa, OK. Since I apparently didn't tell you last night ... I'm God.

God stands up off the couch, as Jeff's coffee machine beeps, indicating it has finished brewing.

**GOD (CONT'D)**
Ah, dude, yes, coffee. Hook it up, man.

God strolls across the living room and takes a seat on one of the bar stools overlooking the kitchen.

Jeff stands dumbfounded in his living room. After a few seconds, Jeff quickly scurries after him into the kitchen and stands directly across the counter-top from him.

**JEFF**
Look, I don't know what your deal is, but you're going to have to leave.

**GOD**
What's the problem?

**JEFF**
How did you get in here?

**GOD**
Yeah, that's a fair question. See, I thought I came in here with you, but, then again, I was fucking hammered last night, so ... your guess is a good as mine, really.

**JEFF**
And (beat) who are you again?

**GOD**
Oh, right, I'm God.

**JEFF**
God?

**GOD**
(Annoyed at having to repeat himself)
Yes, God.

**JEFF**
Yeah, get the fuck out of my apartment!

**GOD**
Whoa, dude, take it easy there. It's pretty goddamn early for this shit.

**JEFF**
There, right there. You can't be God.

**GOD**
What? Why?

**JEFF**
Well, I feel like a idiot even having this conversation, but you can't be God, cos you just said (beat) goddamn.

**GOD**
So?

God is up out of his chair, after concluding that Jeff isn't going to get him any coffee. He walks into the kitchen and starts looking through Jeff's cabinets for a coffee mug.

**JEFF**

So? You took the Lord's name in vain.

**GOD**

What does that mean? (Beat) Where do you keep your coffee cups by the way?

**JEFF**

It means ... like ... you're – damning God, or something.

God turns around to look at Jeff, shrugs.

**GOD**

Well, I don't give a fuck. What's the problem?

God turns back to the cabinets and finds the coffee cups.

**GOD (CONT'D)**

Ooh, here we are. You want any?

God retrieves two cups and pours himself and Jeff a cup of coffee. He hands one to Jeff, who doesn't know how to react.

**JEFF**

Hey! That's my coffee.

**GOD**

And it's fuckin' early. I suggest you drink some.

**JEFF**
All right, this has gone on long enough. I've got to get to work. I don't have time for this shit. Who are you?

God retakes his seat on the bar stool and places his coffee cup on the counter-top, sensing it might be a long haul.

**GOD**
OK. I'm God.

**JEFF**
Fuck off! Who are you?

**GOD**
God.

**JEFF**
Bullshit! Come on. Who the fuck are you?

**GOD**
(Casually shrugs)
Fuckin' God, bro.

**JEFF**
Oh, really? Then how about I see some proof then that you're God.

**GOD**
Sure. Look literally anywhere around you.

**JEFF**
No, none of that. What can you do?

**GOD**
I'm fuckin' God, man. I can do anything.

**JEFF**
All right, well then let's see some shit then.

**GOD**
Like what?

**JEFF**
I don't know, like, some cool shit. You're God, you figure it out.

God breathes out, annoyed, and then focuses in on Jeff's coffee mug. The mug floats out of Jeff's hand and levitates in mid-air. Jeff is admittedly stunned at the sight.

The mug floats about two feet up, right around Jeff's eyes, does a couple flips without spilling a drop of coffee and then the cup slowly comes back down, fitting snugly back into Jeff's hand.

God looks pleased.

**GOD**
See?

**JEFF**
Oh.

**GOD**
(Smugly)
Uh-huh.

**JEFF**
Well, that was ... I mean, I guess.

**GOD**
What do you mean, 'you guess'?!

**JEFF**
Well, I mean, it was all right, I suppose.

**GOD**
What do mean, 'you suppose'?!

**JEFF**
Well, you just sort of lifted my coffee cup, that's really all. It was all right.

**GOD**
Have you ever seen anyone do that before?

**JEFF**
No.

**GOD**
And given that it's whatever the fucking time it is in the morning, and I didn't expect to have to do any of this shit, I think that's pretty good.

**JEFF**
Yeah, it's all right.

**GOD**
It's better than all right, damn it. Can you do that?

**JEFF**
No.

**GOD**
So shut the fuck up, then. (Beat) Geez, tough critic. Give me a fucking break here, man. I just woke up, I'm hungover as shit. I –

**JEFF**
– Wait a minute, so God can get hungover?

God rubs his face. He's getting tired of these types of questions.

**GOD**
Yes.

**JEFF**
So what were you drinking last night then?

**GOD**
Jager.

**JEFF**
God drinks Jager?!

**GOD**

Yes. All these goddamn questions! (Beat) Hey, you got any bacon?

**JEFF**

Whoa, so you eat food?!

**GOD**

Would I be asking you if I didn't? Could you just put two and two together once in a while? Or are we going to be doing this shit the whole damn day?

**JEFF**

Well, you're gonna have to meet me halfway here. This is some pretty weird shit to take in.

**GOD**

Right.

God sips his coffee. It is going to be a long haul.

**JEFF**

All right, so then –

**GOD**

– What?

**JEFF**

Are you omniscient then?

**GOD**

I don't know. What the hell does that mean?

**JEFF**
Do you know everything?
**GOD**
Yeah, but don't make me –

**JEFF**
– So tell me some stuff about me that no one else knows.

**GOD**
Oh, come on. It's too early for this crap. I don't wanna –

**JEFF**
– So you don't know everything?

**GOD**
I do, but it's such a pain in the ass. Sifting through every goddamn thing ever. It sucks man.

**JEFF**
Hey, I'm still very much on the fence, here. You're going to have to prove it, or I still might call the cops or something.

**GOD**
Really? You're really going to make me do this, aren't you? What about the coffee cup? I can do that again.

**JEFF**
Come on.

God's head rolls tiredly around the back of his shoulders. He pauses for a second, then begins.

**GOD**
Jeff Scott. You were conceived in your father's '75 Pontiac Trans Am, you were born on November 13th, 1977 in St Mary's Hospital –

**JEFF**
No, cut to the –

**GOD**
– When you were 13, you went through a brief phase of not wearing any underwear to school. This ended when you mixed up the days when you had gym class, so you made yourself throw up in class and went home sick. You lost your virginity when you were 21, but you have told 14 people that you lost it when you were 18. You have self-diagnosed yourself with cancer 11 times. They were throat, lung, bladder, bowel – that was actually a funny one, because you ate hot wings the night before, and when you shit it out you thought you had bowel cancer. What else? Let's see. Oh, you failed your driver's test four times, but lied about that too. Ooh, the last time you shit your pants was when you were 22 and you weren't even drunk or anything. An epic

story that one was. You once masturbated in a port-o-john in a park when you were 14. You've masturbated watching Rachel Ray 27 times. (beat) One time you were watching porn, drunk, and this one might be my favorite, you became a member of Local Sluts dot com, and were billed a hundred eighty-five dollars before you could cancel it the next day, which was – this is the best part, drumroll please – Christmas Day! What the fuck man?! That's one of the most depressing Christmas Eves, probably ever. In fact, I could actually verify that if you like.

**JEFF**
Nah, that's good. (Beat) You could've just said what my favorite color was or something ... favorite football team, maybe.

**GOD**
Yeah, but that's no fun.

**JEFF**
You know, I really don't masturbate that much, you know. Like from what you said, it sounds like a lot, but –

**GOD**
– We'll just leave it there for now.

Jeff is quiet while the weight of God's information sinks in.

**JEFF**
So you're God then?

**GOD**
Yeah.

**JEFF**
And you exist. That's good to know, I guess.

**GOD**
Yeah, I suppose.

**JEFF**
You know, personally, I never would've guessed it.

**GOD**
Oh right, well that's fine.

**JEFF**
Huh.

**GOD**
Yup.

**JEFF**
Do you want more coffee?

**GOD**
Let's do it up.

God pushes his cup across the counter, while Jeff picks it up and turns to pour God some more coffee. God takes out a cigarette and lights it. Jeff turns back around with a full cup and sets it down in front of God, noticing the cigarette.

**JEFF**
Hey, um, God, you can't smoke in here.

**GOD**
What?

**JEFF**
You can't smoke in here.

**GOD**
Oh, yeah, I know. But this is like, God-smoke. So it's all good.

**JEFF**
Really? Cos it smells just like a cigarette.

**JEFF**
Jeff takes God's cigarette out of his mouth and puts in out in the sink.

**GOD**
Dude, come on. You can't do that.

**JEFF**
Sorry, it's against my building code.

**GOD**
But, I'm God, man. I created all this shit and I can't have a

cigarette? It's not against my building code.

**JEFF**

Not my problem. (Beat) That was for all that Rachel Ray business.

**GOD**

Yeah, fair play. I guess.

**END**

........................................

Luke Wronski is an American comedian, playwright and screenwriter. He describes his work as 'almost exclusively humorous' at this stage of his career. Born in Carlisle, Pennsylvania in 1989, but having spent four years living in the UK, Wronski's comedic style is a mixture of the best of both nations' comedic sensibilities: English, fast-paced wit alongside American outspoken opinions and angst.